REELING IN THE QUEERS

REELING IN THE QUEERS
First published in 2024 by
New Island Books
Glenshesk House
10 Richview Office Park
Clonskeagh
Dublin D14 V8C4
Republic of Ireland

www.newisland.ie

Print ISBN: 978-1-84840-922-4
eBook ISBN: 978-1-84840-923-1

'Two Young Men' by Pearse Hutchinson from *Collected Poems* (2002) is reproduced by kind permission of the author's Estate and The Gallery Press. www.gallerypress.com

The extract from 'A Noise from the Woodshed' by Mary Dorcey is taken from *A Noise from the Woodshed: Short Stories* (Onlywomen, 1989) and is reproduced by kind permission of the author.

Set in 11.5 on 16pt Sabon

Typeset by JVR Creative India
Copyedited by Emma Dunne
Indexed by Eileen O'Neill
Cover design by Emer Brennan, emerbrennan.com
Printed by L&C Printing Group, Poland, lcprinting.eu

New Island Books is a member of Publishing Ireland.

10 9 8 7 6 5 4 3 2 1

REELING IN THE QUEERS

TALES OF IRELAND'S LGBTQ PAST

PÁRAIC KERRIGAN

NEW ISLAND

To the memories of Edmund Lynch and Terri Blanche

We should have known, she said, I mean, recognised it, knowing you were coming back. And of course you should have too and now that she said it you did – recognise the sound. It wasn't, after all, for the want of hearing it. But then other people are different, especially if you haven't heard them speaking or weeping or singing, and anyone can make a mistake about these things, and you had. But now you knew.

—'A Noise from the Woodshed', Mary Dorcey

*Two young men in Belfast fell in love,
hands reaching out in real peace
across the dangerous peace-line.
They gave each other pleasure –
maybe even happiness, who knows? –
and one day the protestant lad
gave his catholic lover
a plant for his window-sill,
a warm geranium.*

—'Two Young Men' (2000), Pearse Hutchinson

Also by Páraic Kerrigan

LGBTQ Visibility, Media and Sexuality in Ireland

Contents

Timeline of Queer Irish History, 1971–2024

1971–72 Gay Liberation Society is founded at Queen's University Belfast.

1973 Establishment of conference on Human Sexuality at the New University of Coleraine in Northern Ireland; Sexual Liberation Movement (SLM) is formed at Trinity College Dublin.

1974 SLM organises the first symposium on homosexuality in the Republic of Ireland at Trinity College Dublin; the Irish Gay Rights Movement (IGRM) is founded; Ireland's first-ever Pride march takes place between the British embassy and the Department of Justice; Cara-Friend helpline is founded to help Northern Ireland's LGBTQ community; the National Gay & Bisexual Helpline (Tel-A-Friend) is set up in the Republic.

1975 Northern Irish Gay Rights Association (NIGRA) is formed; the Phoenix Centre, Dublin's first lesbian and gay community resource, opens at Parnell Square; David Norris is interviewed on RTÉ's *Last House* – the first appearance of an openly gay man in Irish media; Jan Morris, a transgender author, becomes the first transgender person on Irish television, appearing on *The Late Late Show*.

1978   Liberation for Irish Lesbians is formed; Ireland's first trans group, Friends of Eon, is founded by Claire Farrell and Lola; co-founder of the Gate Theatre Micheál Mac Liammóir dies – his funeral is attended by President Éamon de Valera and government ministers and marked a historic moment as they publicly acknowledged and sympathised with Hilton Edwards, Mac Liammóir's life partner, signalling a notable recognition of same-sex relationships.

1978–79 National Gay Federation (NGF) is formed and the Hirschfeld Centre is established on 10 Fownes Street in Temple Bar; the IGRM regroups following collapse in 1977 and opens its own venue, the Phoenix Club, at 18 North Lotts, Bachelors Walk; the first Gay Pride Week celebrations take place in Dublin; secretariat for the International Gay Association is established within the Hirschfeld Centre.

1980   Cork Gay Collective is established; Joni Crone is interviewed by Gay Byrne on RTÉ's *The Late Late Show* – the first appearance of an openly lesbian woman on Irish media; David Norris loses his High Court case to decriminalise homosexuality; Galway Gay Collective is set up; Laurie Steele and Arthur Leahy become the first gay couple interviewed on Irish television.

1981   Jeff Dudgeon wins his case at the European Court of Human Rights (ECHR) in *Dudgeon v the United Kingdom*, leading to the decriminalisation of homosexuality in Northern Ireland; the first National Gay Conference is held in Cork; Liz Noonan becomes the first open and out lesbian to stand for election in Dáil Éireann; UCC refuses recognition to the college's Gay Soc; Ireland's first queer literary journal, *Identity*, is launched by the NGF and edited by independent filmmaker Kieran Hickey; Galway IGRM is established.

1982   Gays Against Imperialism is formed; Gay Defence Committee is founded; gay men Charles Self, John Roche and Declan Flynn are murdered; Dublin Lesbian and Gay Collective is founded; Dublin Lesbian Line is formally named as a dedicated service, having previously been part of Tel-A-Friend; Irish Congress of Trade Unions adopts a motion in support of decriminalisation of homosexuality; Quay Co-Op is established in Cork.

1983   Cork Lesbian Collective is formed; Stop Violence Against Gays and Women (Fairview Park March) takes place following the suspended sentences of Declan Flynn's murderers; Ireland's first large-scale Pride march takes place through the main streets of Dublin; Judith Storm founds the National Transvestite Group and National Transvestite Line; *Women's Community Press* is established, which champions LGBTQ issues; Loafer's Bar opens in Cork; *OUT* magazine is established, the lesbian and gay community's first attempt at a glossy commercial magazine; the Supreme Court upholds the High Court ruling in the Norris case, forcing him to take his case to the ECHR.

1984   RTÉ broadcasts *Access Television*, the first television programme scripted and produced by lesbians and gay men; Cathal Black's *Pigs* becomes one of the first Irish films to include gay representation; Mark Ashton, from Portrush, County Antrim, establishes Lesbians and Gays Support the Miners (LGSM) in London, who supported the National Union Mineworkers Strike in the UK.

1985   Gay Health Action is founded in response to the AIDS crisis; Tonie Walsh becomes the first gay person to stand for election for Dublin City Council; seventy participants attend the world's Second International Gay Youth Congress in Dublin, funded by the Council of Europe; The George opens and is Dublin's first openly gay bar.

1986   Sides dance club is opened on Dame Lane, Dublin, by Kerry man John Nolan, becoming Ireland's first commercial gay venue; *Out for Ourselves: The Lives of Irish Lesbian and Gay Men* is published by the Dublin Lesbian and Gay Men's Collective – the book constitutes Ireland's first collection of coming out stories.

1987   *Gay Community News* is founded by Tonie Walsh and Catherine Glendon; the very first Alternative Miss Ireland takes place; David Norris is elected to Seanad Éireann, becoming the first openly gay member of the Oireachtas; the Hirschfeld Centre burns down and is irrevocably damaged; DJ and major TV personality Vincent Hanley becomes the first high-profile death from an AIDS-related illness in Ireland; Dublin AIDS Alliance (now HIV Ireland) is set up; national AIDS Action Alliance is founded; the GUIDE clinic is established at St James's Hospital, Dublin.

1988   *Norris v Ireland* succeeds at the ECHR, where Ireland's legislation on sex between men is declared unlawful; the Gay and Lesbian Equality Network (GLEN) is founded.

1989   The Prohibition of Incitement to Hatred Act is introduced, one of the first of its kind in the European Union; fifteen people participate in Galway's first Pride parade; UCC finally recognises the university's Gay Soc.

1990   Gay Health Action ceases to operate; lesbian author Mary Dorcey wins the Rooney Prize for Irish Literature; New York's Irish Lesbian and Gay Organisation (ILGO) ask to march in the upcoming St Patrick's Day Parade, but are denied by the Ancient Order of Hibernians.

1991   Lesbians Organising Together (LOT) is founded; Ger Philpott sets up the lobby group AIDSWISE; the first Irish Lesbian and Gay Film Festival takes place in Cork; the first Pride parade takes place in Belfast.

1992   The Gay Men's Health Project (today Gay Men's Health Service) is launched by the Eastern Health Board; Dublin Gay Pride re-emerges following an absence of a number of years; in one of her first public engagements as president, Mary Robinson makes a symbolic gesture and invites lesbian and gay activists to Áras an Uachtaráin; the first LGBTQ float participates in Cork's St Patrick's Day parade, winning a prize; GAZE Film Festival is founded in Dublin; the first known Irish passport is issued to recognise a change of gender.

1993   The Sexual Offences Act introduces a common age of consent of 17, decriminalising sex between men; the Unfair Dismissals Act is amended to include sexual orientation; Dr

Lydia Foy writes to the Registrar of Births requesting a birth certificate to recognise her gender as female.

1994   The Gay Health Network is established.

1995   LinC (Lesbians in Cork) is set up.

1996   *Lesbian and Gay Visions of Ireland, Towards the Twenty-First Century*, edited by Eoin Collins and Íde O'Carroll, is launched by President Mary Robinson in Áras an Uachtaráin; GLEN's *HIV Prevention Strategies and the Gay Community* report is submitted to the Minister for Health and launched by President Robinson in Áras an Uachtaráin, leading to official funding for subsequent initiatives; the Bi Activism group is founded; the first gay kiss on Irish television is broadcast on Irish language soap opera *Ros na Rún*; the Gemini Club is founded, which provided a premises for the trans community; Gerard Stembridge's play *The Gay Detective* premieres.

1997   Dr Lydia Foy begins legal proceedings, having been refused a new birth certificate and legal recognition of her identity as a woman, a process that would take almost two decades.

1998   The Employment Equality Act introduces anti-discrimination measures in employment, meaning that lesbians and gay men cannot be fired on the basis of their sexual identity.

1999   Boyzone star Stephen Gately comes out as gay after *The Sun* newspaper threatens to out him; Sí and the Gemini Club become the first transgender organisations to participate in the Dublin Pride parade; Colm Tóibín's *The Blackwater Lightship* is published, featuring a gay man living with AIDS.

1999-   Brendan Courtney and Alan Hughes become
2000   Ireland's first openly gay television presenters.

2000   The gay male age of consent in Northern Ireland is lowered to 17, bringing it in line with the Republic.

2001   Lesbian Anna Nolan enters the *Big Brother UK* house in the show's first series, eventually coming second.

2002   Brian Dowling, a gay man from Rathangan, County Kildare, wins the second series of *Big Brother UK*; the Equality Authority publishes a significant report on the 'partnership rights' of same-sex couples; Dr Lydia Foy loses her legal case in the High Court.

2003   David Norris attempts to introduce a Civil Partnership Bill, which, although unsuccessful, would spur government parties to finally introduce their own bill seven years later; Belong

To Youth Services is founded; the Emerald Warriors is established, becoming Ireland's first gay rugby team.

2004   Katherine Zappone and Ann Louise Gilligan start the KAL Case, which spurs on the marriage-equality movement in Ireland; Transgender Equality Network of Ireland (TENI) is founded in Cork; the International Dublin Gay Theatre Festival is founded.

2005   Dublin Devils F.C. is formed, becoming Ireland's first gay soccer team.

2006   Taoiseach Bertie Ahern launches the GLEN Strategic Plan; TENI is reformed in Dublin; the LGBTQ community centre Outhouse is founded in Dublin; the first Northwest Pride takes place in County Leitrim; Richard O'Leary and his partner Mervyn Kingston take a legal case against the Department of Social and Family Affairs after the department initially refuses to pay an adult dependent allowance to O'Leary, who was caring for Kingston. After an appeal to the Equality Tribunal, this is overturned.

2007   In the Dr Lydia Foy case in the High Court, Justice Liam McKechnie finds that the Irish State is in contravention of the European Convention of Human Rights on the rights of transgender people. He advises the government to legislate immediately – the government appeals the decision; Limerick hosts its first Pride parade after some years of momentum; LGBT Noise is founded by a small group of volunteers, becoming an independent non-party-political group campaigning for LGBTQ issues, in particular through their annual March for Marriage.

2008   The Immigration, Residence and Protection Bill recognises same-sex couples; the eleven-year-old Irish Queer Archive is transferred to the National Library of Ireland, and the State finally takes ownership of LGBTQ heritage; a High Court judgment holds that a lesbian couple living together in a 'long-term committed relationship of mutual support' should be considered a de facto family under Article 8 of the European Convention of Human Rights.

2009   Marriage Equality is set up to campaign for a referendum on same-sex marriage; GAA player Dónal Óg Cusack comes out as gay, becoming the first high-profile Irish sportsperson to do so.

2010   The Civil Partnership and Cohabitants Act is introduced, granting civil partnership to same-sex couples; the government sets up an inter-departmental committee on the legal recognition of transgender people on foot of a High Court recommendation in Dr Lydia

Foy's case; LGBT Ireland is established by seven local LGBT helplines.

2011   Jerry Buttimer, Dominic Hannigan and John Lyons become the first openly gay elected TDs in Dáil Éireann; the Gay Health Network and the Health Services Executive (HSE) launch Ireland's first-ever National HIV Prevention and Sexual Health Awareness Programme for men who have sex with men (MSM); Louise Hannon becomes the first transgender person to use the Employment Equality Act to win a case against an employer on the grounds of gender discrimination; Senator David Norris makes a bid for the Irish presidency.

2012   The final Alternative Miss Ireland contest takes place; Belong To Youth Services unveil LGBT Youth Mental Health Ireland, supporting LGBTQ youths around the country to develop positive mental health; Bi+ Ireland network is founded.

2013   The government-established Constitutional Convention overwhelmingly recommends a referendum on same-sex marriage; Yes Equality is established by GLEN, Marriage Equality and the Irish Council for Civil Liberties (ICCL).

2014   'Pantigate' emerges as a national scandal, resulting in Panti Bliss's viral noble call speech in the Abbey Theatre; Maria Walsh comes out as a lesbian after being crowned the Rose of Tralee.

2015 An overwhelming 'yes' vote in the Marriage Equality Referendum; during the referendum campaign, then Minister for Health Leo Varadkar comes out; the Gender Recognition Act is passed – Ireland becomes only the fourth country in the world to pass and enact gender recognition based on self-determination; Equality Minister Aodhán Ó Ríordáin introduces a bill to remove Section 37 of the Employment Equality Act, 1998, which had a 'religious ethos' exemption allowing employers to fire or refuse to hire LGBTQ people; iconic queer venue The Dragon closes; Tomás Heneghan brings a High Court challenge against Ireland's lifetime ban on blood donation by MSM; high-profile GAA player Valerie Mulcahy comes out as gay.

2016 Katherine Zappone is the first open and out lesbian to become a government minister; Belfast youth worker Ellen Murray is the first transgender person to bid for a seat in the Northern Ireland Assembly; Teach Solais is launched in Galway, becoming the west's first LGBTQ centre; David Parris takes a case against Trinity College Dublin to the Court of Justice of the European Union regarding survivor's pension eligibility for his partner and not being able to avail of it. The European Court rules that Parris was not treated unfairly and that Ireland was not mandated to apply retrospective measures.

2017   Leo Varadkar becomes the first openly gay Taoiseach and only the fifth openly gay head of government in the world.

2018   The world's first National LGBTI+ Youth Strategy is published by the Irish government; the government review of the Gender Recognition Act 2015 recommends access for non-binary people under 18 with parental consent; Ryan O'Shaughnessy's Eurovision Song Contest entry 'Together' is Ireland's first Eurovision entry to depict a same-sex couple during a live performance, becoming censored in China; Leo Varadkar issues an apology to the Irish LGBTQI+ people who had faced discrimination and suffering at the hands of the Irish State prior to the decriminalisation of homosexuality in 1993; Sporting Pride is founded, becoming Ireland's national body to get LGBTQ people more active in sport.

2019   The National LGBTI+ Inclusion Strategy 2019–2021 is published; Equality for Children is founded to fight for the rights of a child in a same-sex family to have a legally recognised relationship with both of their parents.

2020   Same-sex marriage is legalised in Northern Ireland; Na Gaeil Aeracha is founded, becoming the world's first LGBTQ+ GAA team.

2021   The government establishes the Working Group to Examine the Disregard of Convictions for Certain Qualifying Offences Related to Consensual Sexual Activity between Men in Ireland.

2023   The Working Group on Disregard's final report is submitted to the government; Taoiseach Leo Varadkar unveils Ireland's first AIDS memorial in the People's Park in the Phoenix Park.

2024   Rebecca Tallon de Havilland becomes Ireland's first transgender television presenter; non-binary artist Bambi Thug becomes Ireland's entrant for the Eurovision Song Contest; Senator David Norris retires – he holds the record for the longest continuous period of service in the Seanad; Andrew Muir becomes the first openly gay minister in Northern Ireland's Assembly as Minister for Agriculture, Environment and Rural Affairs, while Kenneth Blair becomes the first gay Deputy Speaker in Northern Ireland's Assembly; Taoiseach Leo Varadkar resigns from office and as leader of Fine Gael.

Introduction

The story of LGBTQ liberation in Ireland has, arguably, been one of progress, with significant milestones such as the success of the 'yes' vote in the same-sex marriage referendum and the passing of the Gender Recognition Act in 2015. Two years later in 2017, Ireland saw the ascension of a biracial, openly gay son of an immigrant, Leo Varadkar, as the country's Taoiseach. These events positioned Ireland as a bastion of progressive social change, cementing its status as 'an island at the centre of the world' and demonstrating a huge change of heart for what was once a staunchly Catholic country.[1] Significantly, this progress has been considered a culmination of transformative social change catalysed and nurtured by an array of LGBTQ activism and events since the founding of varying Irish gay civil rights movements across 1973 and 1974.

Within the grand and emerging narrative of LGBTQ Ireland, however, are woven intricate threads of ordinary people's extraordinary stories. This book aims to tell the lesser-told tales of Ireland's LGBTQ community: stories of those who believed in change and stories of those who simply wanted to have fun. Within LGBTQ archives across Ireland, in the warm kitchens of people's homes, via Zoom grids and across shared coffees in city cafés are an array of vibrant tales. This book attempts to reel some of them in.

In the summer of 2022 I was speaking with a friend, Rita Wild, who had spent some years as an activist and volunteer with the Belfast lesbian community. I had mentioned to her that I was writing a history of lesser-told stories in Irish LGBTQ life. With a raised eyebrow, she mentioned once being on a bus 'full of lesbians' driving from Belfast all the way to Cork and Galway, as part of a Lesbian Line exchange. This piqued my interest, and Rita told me she would see if her old Belfast 'comrades' would be interested in talking to me. A number of days later Rita contacted me to share their details, giving me the go-ahead to reach out. She sent a follow-up voice note on WhatsApp to tell me 'they're very happy, but really amused' that someone was interested in this story so many years on. I reached out, hoping to hear about their experiences, stories and memories of their work with the Belfast Lesbian Line and their exchanges with the lesbian community across the island of Ireland. One person in particular, Claire Hackett, was very enlivened by my request. She responded to my email confirming she would participate, but noting, 'if we realised we were making history, we might have kept better records'.[2]

This exchange with the former activists of the Belfast lesbian community and the Lesbian Line speaks to the core of *Reeling in the Queers*, its focus on the significance of ordinary LGBTQ people who did extraordinary things. While many in Ireland's LGBTQ community may not have changed laws, their actions provided hope, relief, support and, crucially, created enclaves of fun and queer joy.

The imagination and political and cultural consciousness of Irish queer life has, to varying degrees, been captured within the various LGBTQ archives held across the island – their very existence demonstrating a growing conscientiousness around documenting queer life in Ireland. From Edmund Lynch's newspaper cuttings of any mention of 'homosexuality' in the 1970s to the consolidation of the community's activities in what would become the Irish Queer Archive, the Irish LGBTQ community has always tried to make queer life in Ireland intelligible. While the Irish Queer Archive served as a significant repository, the Cork LGBT Archive, the Irish Trans Archive, the GCN Archive, the LGBT History Northern Ireland Archive and the Irish LGBT Oral History Archive have together allowed me to connect with previous generations and pluck at the finer threads of cultural, political and social life in LGBTQ Ireland. In saying that, the stories of some of the people in this book cannot be found in archives, but rather are waiting to be told in personal documents and memory.

While *Reeling in the Queers* harnesses queer archives, oral history interviews trace the contours of diverse queer life. Being connected with these individuals, who, like me, faced various forms of discrimination due to their LGBTQ identity, underscored the shared experiences that span generations. The intergenerational dialogue of the oral histories not only serves as a bridge between the past and the present but also provides a conduit through which previously unknown lives and stories can be heard and understood.

I use the term 'queer' in a broad sense, encompassing various sexual orientations and gender identities that differ from the heterosexual norm and those identifying with the gender they were assigned at birth. 'Queer' is particularly useful when discussing a wide array of cultural practices, as well as when addressing same-sex attraction or gender diversity in historical periods and locations where these practices and identities were not defined as they are today. 'Queer' enables us to explore the lives and relationships of people in the past without imposing our contemporary experiences or frames of reference onto theirs. I am also conscious of how 'queer' originated as a derogatory insult. My own experience of growing up and going to school in the late 1990s and 2000s saw this evolve to the term 'gay' being harnessed and deployed to insult and taunt. The 1980s and 1990s saw activists reclaiming 'queer', often used to abuse and humiliate, and turning it towards empowerment and radicalisation against something that was once associated with stigma and shame.

In 1861 the Victorian morality legislation, the Offences Against the Persons Act, while abolishing the death penalty for 'buggery', retained its illegality around sex between men and would remain on the statute books until the last decade of the twentieth century.

This legislation is significant, as the criminality that emerged from it resulted in a climate of homophobia for many years after. The 1970s later witnessed the emergence of gay civil rights movements, notably the Sexual Liberation Movement in 1973, the Northern Ireland Gay Rights Association (NIGRA) in 1975 and the Irish Gay Rights Movement (IGRM) in 1974, the latter of which established forms of queer socialisation and Ireland's first designated queer space in the form of the Phoenix Club. While the IGRM later imploded as a result of in-fighting and personality clashes, the National Gay Federation, formed in 1979, founded the Hirschfeld Centre at 10 Fownes Street in Dublin's Temple Bar, which would bring queer nightlife to a whole new level through the dance club Flikkers while providing a raft of other social services and resources.

In 1982 Jeff Dudgeon, a Belfast shipping clerk, successfully petitioned the European Court of Human Rights to extend the partial decriminalisation of male homosexuality to Northern Ireland. But the 1980s would also see the vulnerability of queer life exposed through the murders of Charles Self in his home in 1982 and Declan Flynn later that year, followed by John Porter in Cork in 1983. The Charles Self murder investigation saw a campaign mounted by the gardaí to collect information and details around Dublin's gay community. The five perpetrators of Declan Flynn's murder received suspended sentences, sparking outrage within the queer community and a notable public protest in the form of the Fairview Park March and the Pride Protest March.

The 1980s witnessed the emergence of the AIDS crisis, which was confronted by a number of groups such as Gay Health Action (GHA) in 1985, ACT UP in 1990 and AIDSWISE in 1991. Simultaneously, the Campaign for Homosexual Law Reform, established in 1977 took a challenge to the laws criminalising gay sex acts between men. Led by Irish gay rights pioneer David Norris, the case failed at the Irish High Court in 1977 and Supreme Court in 1983, until eventually it succeeded at the European Court of Human Rights in 1988. Now that Ireland was mandated by Europe to decriminalise, gay law reform became a key issue and saw groups such as the Gay and Lesbian Equality Network (GLEN) emerge in 1988 to campaign for it, eventually finding success when homosexuality was decriminalised in 1993. Transgender activism also burgeoned during the decade: in April 1997 Dr Lydia Foy began legal proceedings having been refused a new birth certificate and legal recognition of her female gender in 1993.

The year 2024 marks half a century since the founding of the IGRM, along with Ireland's first Gay Pride event, all the way back in 1974. This serves as the perfect juncture to look back at the impact of Ireland's LGBTQ community on politics, society and culture. The stories, times and topics that this book traverses are by no means a complete history of Ireland's LGBTQ community, but they do present a window into different aspects of queer Irish culture. While emphasis is often placed on the political aspects of LGBTQ life, in terms of legislative progress and successes, this book also points towards how forms of queer cultural production, socialisation and fun were as crucial to LGBTQ life as political legitimation.

Reeling in the Queers takes inspiration from RTÉ's beloved television series *Reeling in the Years*. Just as each episode of that show revisits the events of a specific year through archival footage, reflecting on their contemporary relevance in shaping Ireland, this book aims to do the same by reeling in the stories of LGBTQ individuals, events and figures: stories that have left an indelible mark not just on the queer community but also on modern-day Ireland; stories that bear witness to the resilience of queer culture, a testament to how it emerged and thrived against all odds and the people who made it happen.

1

'The Two Mothers Got Together and Sorted It Out'

*Phil Moore, Parents Enquiry and
Gay Law Reform*

In April 1989 Phil Moore, a mother of two from Dartry Park in South Dublin, is sitting among the audience of *The Late Late Show*, then Ireland's most popular television programme. The evening of joyous candour, with prompted laughter from the studio manager and the potential to interact with one of Ireland's biggest stars, Gay Byrne, as he interviews a host of celebrities, is wasted on Phil. Instead, she is anxious, then becomes frustrated and is finally furious.

Tonight's special edition of *The Late Late Show* features a debate around homosexuality and whether Ireland should decriminalise homosexual acts. The Irish government had just been mandated to do so after David Norris's Campaign for Homosexual Law Reform was successful in the European Court of Human Rights (ECHR) a year earlier, in 1988. On the panel, Paddy Monaghan, from the conservative reactionary group

Christians Concerned, explains to the studio audience that it isn't 'normal for a man to be preoccupied with another man's back passage'.[1] This anti-gay, anti-decriminalisation discourse gains traction when another member of the panel, Máire Kirrane of the Irish conservative advocacy group Family Solidarity, speaks from her position as a mother, stating that she is concerned about how impressionable children are to being influenced by gay people, before claiming that there are in fact 'very few actual homosexuals' and that they are an 'aberration' to the 'law of God'.[2]

Phil at this point has heard enough. She is the mother of a gay son herself and can no longer stand to hear members of the panel referring to her child as an aberration. Feeling enraged, she intervenes in the debate, declaring to the studio audience and those watching at home that 'when you are talking about my child, he is wonderful and perfectly normal. It is nothing that he can grow out of, because if a mother says that to a child, that means you're not accepting him.'[3] And it was the love of a mother for her gay son that would lead to one of the most significant shifts in the rights for LGBTQ people in Ireland. Phil Moore was to become an important proponent in implementing gay law reform in 1993 – yet her contribution has not always received the credit that it deserves. This is the story of how a mother changed the course of gay liberation in Ireland, not to mention helping many Irish families along the way.

Born in Dublin in 1933 – only a year after the 31st International Eucharistic Congress, a landmark event demonstrating the powerful influence of the Catholic Church in the State – Phil Moore was of a generation that grew up in an Ireland that was staunchly conservative, entrenched in the moral habitus and ethos of the Church. Having married Harry, a stereo salesman who worked on Dawson Street, the couple carved out a life for themselves and their family in Dartry Park. Phil describes her politics throughout her life as feminist and relatively liberal, but the question of gay identities had never crossed her mind.

That remained the case until, one lunchtime, her sixteen-year-old son Dermod walked into the kitchen. As Phil was sitting at the kitchen table eating a bowl of lentil soup, Dermod said, 'Ma, I've something to tell you that I don't think you'll like. I'm gay.' Phil was taken aback – this she had not been expecting. Relieved that her teenage son hadn't got himself into trouble, she replied, 'Oh, you're only 16! You'll grow out of it. You couldn't possibly know.'[4]

Following that initial conversation, as her lentil soup cooled in the bowl, and in the weeks thereafter, Phil's mind raced with endless possibilities. She was frightened for her son's future. Would he be lonely? Would he ever be happy? Would he be bullied? Would he be beaten up? Would he have secret love affairs? Phil describes 'drowning in a huge wave of misery and fear … not realising that there were so many horrible myths and prejudices in my mind concerning gay people'.[5] Phil began to understand that what she was feeling was a manifestation of institutionalised homophobia, growing up in conservative Catholic Ireland, as she described it, 'a compound of all the music hall jokes imbibed in a lifetime'.[6] With her son's brave disclosure, his choosing to reveal a crucial part of his identity, Phil says that, 'out on the ground and then out of my pores came prejudices that I didn't even think I had'.[7] This served as a turning point for Phil, who realised that 'you have to take out all these myths and prejudices till you suddenly find out that if there's a problem with being gay, it's the parents' problem'.[8] Dermod was still the same boy she had raised, and being gay was just part of who he was. So from there on in, together with her husband, she set out to understand what life was like for young gay people in Ireland.

By this stage Dermod was active in the National Gay Federation's Youth Group, Ireland's first gay youth organisation, which operated out of the Hirschfeld Centre on 10 Fownes Street in Dublin's Temple Bar every Sunday from 3 p.m. to 6 p.m. For many young people, the youth group was a lifeline, and simply meeting other lesbian and gay people of the same age, who understood the complexity of living as a young gay person in Ireland, was extremely rewarding.[9] One of the Sundays when Dermod was going to the youth group, Phil and Harry asked if they could join, with the aim of understanding a little bit more about his new world and to get a sense of the community he had built for himself at the Hirschfeld. The young gay and lesbian people there began to confide in this warm, sympathetic older couple: 'Now, the stories we heard from some of these kids broke my heart. I was really anxious about these kids who were thrown out of their houses, their fathers beat them up, their mothers packing their case saying, "I don't want to see you again." Harry and I looked at each other and said, "This is not right."[10]

From that point onwards, Phil's concern for her son and his friends evolved into activism. She started to speak out on radio chat shows, particularly in debates around homosexuality, where she would come on air and declare 'my son is not a criminal'. On one occasion, the Fine Gael politician Mary Banotti rang her in tears after hearing her on the radio. As his mother's profile grew, Dermod Moore became known in the media as 'the gay with the parents' – the exception to the rule, such was the climate and culture around gay identity at the time. This was also when Phil decided that her time as the only mother of a gay son would come to an end.

The stories of hardship experienced by young gays and lesbians, coupled with the tumultuous reactions of their parents, inspired Phil to develop a much-needed voluntary support group for parents, which became known as Parents Enquiry. The story of Parents Enquiry stretches back to its original founder, Rose Robertson, who was a special operations executive for the Allies in Nazi-occupied France during World War II. She was lodged with two young male French Resistance agents, whom she discovered in an embrace one night. Not knowing a thing about homosexuality, Robertson eventually asked them about it, only to discover stories of family prejudice and rejection.[11] She was deeply shocked at the extent to which parents could be so cruel towards their own children. Much later, in 1965, Robertson took in two young male lodgers, who by chance were lovers, and once again heard stories of their parents' homophobic attitudes. This finally prompted Robertson to set up Parents Enquiry, which she ran from her home in London for three decades. Travelling to give workshops was central to Robertson's role, and the NGF brought her to speak in the Hirschfeld Centre in 1981, which was where Phil met her and became inspired to set up an Irish chapter of the organisation.

Collaborating with a number of other parents, including Patricia Kilroy, who became a long-standing ally of Phil's within Parents Enquiry, the organisation advocated for gay youths who did not necessarily have a platform to speak for themselves, regularly issuing press releases to garner airtime on radio and column inches in papers. In an article in *The Irish Times*, for example, Phil argued that 'parents have to get their priorities right. They have to reconcile themselves to the sexual preferences and needs of their children.'[12] On one occasion she harnessed connections she had made in the feminist movement and asked Terry Prone to come down to the Hirschfeld Centre to meet the youths and their parents for her weekly column. This media visibility began to have significant ramifications. Having heard Phil on the radio one day, a mother who was struggling with their child coming out asked her son: 'I know there's a parents' thing, I don't know who's involved, but take me to the Hirschfeld.' So he did, and the evening the mother arrived happened to be Flikkers night, the regular disco at the Hirschfeld. And while the sight of gay men and women dancing together to The Pointer Sisters might have been an overload for a mother coming to terms with her gay son, this one simply looked around her and said, 'Oh my God, you're all so happy here.'[13] Just hearing Phil on the radio had brought one mother closer to her son's world, and she subsequently danced the night away with him.

While engendering visibility was a central part of her work, what took up most of her time was travelling around the country and actually meeting parents. To a degree, Phil's life became like that of a doctor on-call. People would ring her at all hours and also approach her in the Hirschfeld Centre, asking if she would meet them privately. Usually she would do this in a pub, or Bewley's on Grafton Street if they were based in Dublin. They would then tell Phil their stories and their fears for their child. 'I always felt that [when] any parent [...] reached out to another parent, there was hope for the child,'[14] she says.

There was a huge personal cost to doing this work. On one occasion, Phil was at home getting ready for a family celebration for her and Harry's twenty-fifth wedding anniversary when, as guests began to arrive, her preparations were interrupted by a phone call from a distressed mother explaining that 'my daughter has just told me she is gay, I don't know what to do, my world has fallen in'.[15] And so, as the party started, Phil spoke to that mother, telling her that her daughter was still the same person and that all she needed to do was love her.

The young gay people in the NGF Youth Group would often call on Phil to serve as a mediator between them and their parents. One young girl who had just come out as lesbian pleaded with Phil to come to her home and speak with her mother, which she did on a roasting hot day in their back garden, where a chocolate cake sat on the table, melting in the sun. Central for Phil in interactions such as these, between parent and child, was time and for both sides to be patient. When that young girl nervously approached Phil later that week to see how the meeting had gone with her mother, Phil gently told her that all was well but to 'give your parents time. I'm asking for a mature reaction from you as a young person [...] You've taken a few years to come to terms with it, give your parents a little time.'[16] Not only was Phil mediating between a parent and their young gay or lesbian child, but she was also mediating between the parents and the homophobically charged society in which they were raised.

This work was key to Phil's career and activism – in terms of bringing parents along to align themselves with reform and understanding, enabling a version of their family that included a gay son or daughter. Years of time and personal sacrifice were devoted to speaking with families, and much of this work would eventually coalesce more explicitly around the sphere of politics, where Phil would become central to the cause of gay law reform. Following David Norris's successful case at the ECHR, the Irish government was mandated to implement gay law reform, yet from the time of the ruling in 1988, various governments refused to prioritise the issue. The newly formed Gay and Lesbian Equality Network (GLEN) set out to ensure that the government would implement gay law reform, through which Phil and Parents Enquiry often offered to lend support. The 1993 election resulted in a Fianna Fáil–Labour coalition: a government and a new Minister for Justice, Máire Geoghegan-Quinn, that were open to potentially changing the law.

GLEN had lobbied Geoghegan-Quinn and worked with the Department of Justice, and they were veering towards full law reform with an equal age of consent.[17] However, things were still uncertain, and a delegation representing the community was formed by GLEN, who asked Phil to join what would be a final conversation with the minister – the hope being that, if all else failed, Phil might be able to get through to her.

Walking into government buildings in 1993, Minister Geoghegan-Quinn shook the hands of each member of the delegation: Kieran Rose, Suzy Byrne, Christopher Robson and, finally, Phil. The minister looked oddly at Phil and was demonstrably unsure as to why was she was with the gay delegation. Each member subsequently said their piece, as the minister took down vigorous notes, but when it came to Phil, she put down her pen and just looked at her. Phil somehow knew that they were about to talk frankly: 'Now, I didn't preach at her. I just talked about Dermod, how funny and nice he was and then about the plight that young gay people go through with their parents ... I spoke to her from mother to mother.'[18] In that moment, Phil's years of activism and experience as a mother shifted something in the minister, who had been experiencing resistance in the Fianna Fáil parliamentary party. Minister Geoghegan-Quinn recalls how Phil's disclosures in their meeting were central to confronting this resistance at one of the parliamentary party meetings prior to the passing of the reform bill:

'Okay, I'm looking around the room and the vast majority of my colleagues here are men. The vast majority of you are married and a substantial number of you have teenage sons, so let me paint a picture for you' and I painted the picture Phil Moore painted for me. 'Your son is nineteen, twenty, twenty-one. He comes in and tells you he is gay. And what do you do? You do the rounds, you go to the priest and doctors and all the rest of it and at the end of the day, are you going to say to him that just because he is gay and different you are going to throw him out?'[19]

Not one person in the room said anything and later, on 24 June 1993, Máire Geoghegan-Quinn passed the legislation that finally decriminalised homosexuality. She then walked straight across the Dáil chamber to the public gallery and shook the hand of each person, including Phil, who was eagerly waiting in the wings watching the bill being passed. As Phil recalls today, that initial conversation was 'the turning point; she had sons of her own. She said this was it, and she kept saying it. She said I was crucial in that meeting. It was the two mothers, no question about it. That was the two Irish mothers [who] got together and sorted it out.'[20]

Gay Pride 1993 happened the day after the passing of the legislation – and to no one's surprise, it celebrated the decriminalisation of homosexuality in Ireland as the community joyously chanted through the streets, 'What do we want? Law reform! When did we get it? Yesterday!' And Phil Moore walked alongside them. Taking in the sheer jubilation, she watched as the community she had worked so hard with danced and chanted through the streets, celebrating that they were no longer criminals. As the parade ended at the Central Bank, just off Dame Street, members of the community started speaking to the gathered crowd. At one point Phil was called up to the stage to give an address. A friend beside her said, 'Phil, they're calling you!' Phil turned to her, in all her modesty and humility, and simply said, 'I know. But I'm going home. It's theirs now, it's theirs now. I've done my bit.'

Even though much of Phil's work with parents and their gay and lesbian children took place in the 1980s and 1990s, the ramifications of her work and legacy stretch to the present day. Only recently, over thirty years after giving a public lecture in UCD, she was approached by a woman who told her, 'I was a very lonely lesbian in UCD and I heard you speak. You saved my life.' Another young man stopped her on the street to tell her she was crucial in helping his mother accept his sexuality. 'You're my hero for what you did for my mother,' he said.[21] Phil's response is always that of a humane, generous and utterly humble individual. 'They were all heroes themselves,' she likes to say.

Phil Moore's activism and work, and that of many others such as Patricia Kilroy in Parents Enquiry, cannot be overstated. The institution of motherhood – and of Irish motherhood in particular – demonstrated how an 'old order' could realign with new values and beliefs and how mothers could become staunch allies in the fight for gay rights. What Phil said and did opened up the Irish family as a place of inclusivity and one that could welcome gay and lesbian children. She not only helped one family at a time, but she also used the power of motherhood and a mother's love for her gay child to change the laws criminalising homosexuality. Phil Moore's story is not exclusively relevant to a certain period of Ireland's LGBTQ history on its journey to liberation: it has a transcendental message for people today, particularly for those parents coming to terms with a child who has come out or who might do so in the future. For those parents, I would like to conclude with Phil's words: 'If your child approaches you and says, "I'm gay," I hope you realise that what they are asking is, "Will you still love me even though I'm gay?"'[22]

2

Out of the Closet and into a Boy Band

*4Guyz and the Pursuit of
1990s Pop Stardom*

In the mid 1990s the manufactured boy band had become a significant cultural touchstone and a mainstream success story that dominated the charts across the UK and Ireland. UK-based Take That, for example, ended 1995 with a string of massive hits, which included 'Back for Good' and 'Never Forget'. Irish pop legend Louis Walsh's own locally created group Boyzone, despite a tentative beginning with questionable dance moves on their launch on *The Late Late Show* in 1993, had achieved mainstream success by 1995, with their album *Said and Done* becoming a breakout hit and reaching the top of the charts in the UK and Ireland. Boyzone in particular had established a significant gay fan base in Ireland, and their smash hit 'Love Me for a Reason' became an anthem for the community when the band played in the Parliament Inn, a popular gay venue.[1] Queer publication *Gay Community News* (*GCN*), however, questioned Boyzone's dedication to their gay Irish fan base when it speculated that the boy band pulled out of an appearance at the Playground, a newly opened gay venue, in 1994, potentially because 'they couldn't be bothered about their gay fans'.[2] Boyzone's ambiguous relationship with their gay fans would become a source of contention for would-be pop-band manager in the making Junior Larkin.

Junior Larkin was best known in the early 1990s as the drag queen Kylie O'Reilly, a one-time member of Ireland's Kylie Kavern, a drag-queen house venerating Kylie Minogue. In his guise as Kylie O'Reilly, he entered a song (unsuccessfully) into the National Song Contest called 'Delicious Boyz (Lick Me I'm Delicious)' and hosted talent search events such as 'Search for a Star' in Dublin's premier gay bar, The George. By day, Junior worked in *GCN*, and after a year there he established his own free gay magazine, *Guyz*. While getting *Guyz* off the ground, Junior sought to interview Boyzone in the hopes of increasing the profile of the magazine. However, he quickly found the boy band's press officers frustratingly evasive and was consistently fobbed off by them. This led him to the conclusion that Boyzone's press officer did not want to acknowledge their gay fan base and saw him playfully suggesting that a gay boy band, designed for and by the community that would truly honour their gay fan base, was needed.[3] While initially a reactionary proposal, made in the heat of the moment, Junior's idea for a gay-oriented band was picked up by some of his friends in the newspaper industry. The idea was dubbed

Gayzone, which emerged as an early tabloid moniker for what would become a new entertainment enterprise. As Junior argued, 'Boy bands are very popular in the gay community and we want to give a boy band to the gay community who will acknowledge their gay fans and play the gay clubs.'[4] The hype and interest from Junior's initial idea would eventually snowball into the formation of the aptly named 4Guyz, Ireland's first openly gay boy band, and one of the first in the world. 4Guyz were significant because they were part of the LGBTQ community and budding pop stars in an industry where there was an innate fear that coming out or being gay or queer in a boy band would irreparably damage any hope of a career or market success.

With fire in his belly to create Ireland's new pop sensation, Junior enlisted the help of Dublin-based club and concert promoter John Pickering to get the band together, and an advertisement was placed in *Guyz* magazine looking for 'young men under 23, with good body/looks and the ability to sing and dance'. On 8 February 1996, sixty gay (and some straight) pop hopefuls attended auditions in the Ormond Multimedia Centre.[5] Over the course of the auditions, the contestants were whittled down until a five-piece emerged that 'gelled really quickly and worked really well together': Karl Anderson, Keith Lee, John McGurke, Mark Power and Ken Quinn.[6] The five-person line-up seemed somewhat jarring for a band that signified four members in its name, but Junior Larkin had selected the name prior to the establishment of the final line-up, and was loath to change it when the five gelled. Mark Power comments that 4Guyz did not literally mean that there were four members, but that the band was aimed at the proverbial 'guys' on the gay scene, noting that 'a lot of people missed that bit, they just thought the Irish couldn't count'.[7]

The concept of the boy band originated in the United States in the 1960s and 1970s, with The Temptations and The Jackson 5, followed by The Osmonds, and then crossing the Atlantic to the UK in the shape of Wham! in the 1980s, followed by a spate of manufactured boy bands in the 1990s.[8] The marketing of the boy band as a cultural archetype (during the 1990s in particular) was designed to appeal to gay sensibilities, both visually and performatively. Often, these bands were deliberately marketed towards a gay audience. Take That, for example, began their career through promotion on the gay circuit, and the music video for their début single 'Do What U Like' saw the five-piece cavorting around and breakdancing, half-naked and covered in jelly and custard. Similarly, Boyzone's promotional material, with their perfectly coiffed hair, smooth complexions and styling, constructed a gay-friendly appeal, especially in their first single, 'Working My Way Back to You', which featured muscle vests and billowing shirts. Boy bands appealed to a gay audience through these marketing strategies and stylistic approaches, while also making the gay community feel seen and represented through these homoerotic subtexts. In fact, as Mark Power commented just after 4Guyz's formation, 'At least we don't have to suppress our sexuality, but gay members of other boy bands might struggle to do so.'[9] Indeed, it wasn't until 1999 that Stephen Gately of Boyzone came out as gay, after being forced to do so by a tabloid, such was his fear of the ramifications of his sexual identity on the band's success.

Assured and confident as a gay band, 4Guyz were quickly put to work with a gruelling schedule designed to sculpt them into a pop act that would not only be entertaining live but could also compete in the music charts. Their regimen consisted of morning sessions at the gym, from 10 to 11.45 a.m., followed by twelve minutes on the sunbeds to work on their tans, then singing lessons with a vocal coach lasting from midday to 1 p.m., followed by an afternoon of dance classes with their choreographer, Eddie McGuinness, from 2 to 5 p.m. in the famous Digges Lane Dance Centre.[10] It was here that the band came into contact with many of the successful Irish pop groups of the era, including B*Witched, Boyzone and OTT.[11] All of this work was to get the band ready for their launch night in the new gay venue run by Junior Larkin at Wonderbar in the Ormond Multi-Media Centre on 22 March 1996. The run-up saw 4Guyz developing as an autonomous performing unit, creating a vocal style and carving out a presence on the gay circuit before seeking a recording deal. They quickly began developing a cover version of Diana Ross's gay anthem 'I'm Coming Out' as their demo, along with a rendition of The Weather Girls' 'It's Raining Men' and Gloria Gaynor's 'I Am What I Am' for their début gig.[12]

The launch of the band was no understated affair, with managers Larkin and Pickering creating a significant media buzz and securing a segment on the cult magazine show *Eurotrash* on Channel 4 in the UK, presented by Jean Paul Gaultier and Antoine de Caunes and a hallmark of 1990s British television. The international début on *Eurotrash* launched 4Guyz into the national spotlight, while also positioning their gay politics front and centre in terms of the band's marketing. As John McGurke noted, 'We're already saying that we're gay, just so in five months there wouldn't be any hassle, and if we do get famous, people won't go off us by finding out we're gay.' The *Eurotrash* appearance markedly pointed out how homosexuality had been a crime in Ireland a number of years ago and that 'now young, free and legal, 4Guyz are hoping that the mainstream audience is ready to embrace them'.[13]

The band's début gig at Wonderbar created a significant buzz; they were slated to appear with American singer Lonnie Gordon, who rose to fame in the 1990s through her collaboration with fabled producers Stock Aitken Waterman.[14] The launch night exceeded expectations and they were soon getting plenty of gigs. The novelty of being a gay band became fodder for the press, with John Pickering showing a particular talent for garnering tabloid space. This, along with the *Eurotrash* appearance, piqued the interest of the gay circuit in the UK, with 4Guyz following Take That's initial marketing strategy of performing to gay audiences and Prides across the UK, as well as in Berlin and Gran Canaria. Their success was cemented with the group landing the coveted cover of the UK's *Gay Times* magazine for its June 1996 edition.

While 4Guyz may have been representative of a burgeoning confidence for gay people in post-decriminalisation Ireland, the band's overtly gay identity proved too much for certain pockets of conservative Ireland, who sometimes resisted giving any visibility to the band by refusing them a platform on the basis that they were gay. Such was the case with the annual Rose of Tralee International Festival, which the *Sunday Independent* announced with the headline 'Gay Band Get Rose Week Ban'.[15] The band's co-manager John Pickering had been attempting to get 4Guyz onto the slate of performing acts for the week-long festival, but was declined at every opportunity by the organising committee. The newspapers speculated that this was because of the innate conservatism of the festival and also, while Dublin may be more comfortable with gay people, the rural setting was not as welcoming: 'They've been accepted so well and it would be nice to see things go as well for them down the country as they have in Dublin.'[16] 4Guyz also criticised the festival committee's general conservatism, particularly around the Rose of Tralee's treatment of women, with a statement saying, 'Fresh from insulting Irish women at last year's Rose of Tralee, thanks to their Victorian attitudes to unmarried mothers, the festival committee has struck again,'[17] criticising the festival policy that no unmarried mothers were permitted to enter the contest – a rule which, astonishingly, remained in place until 2008. In that sense, their minoritised status and treatment at the hands of the Rose of Tralee festival enabled 4Guyz to confront what they considered misogynistic policies around entry. Conversely, band member Mark Power later noted that the band had excellent PR and that the Rose of Tralee 'incident' could possibly have been embellished by the band's management to ensure column inches and coverage.

The very existence of a public, out-and-proud gay boy band was harnessed as a source of debate across the media in Ireland. 4Guyz would regularly appear on radio shows alongside a politician or an individual from a conservative Christian group who would say 'you shouldn't be allowed to do this', 'this is filth' and 'it's a sin'.[18] Panel discussions involved claims that 4Guyz were 'disgracefully' and 'unnecessarily' flaunting their sexuality, often with the band in the studio for the barrage of criticism. The band's usual retort to this reactionary resistance was the simple claim that they were only flaunting happy songs. Yet that very claim and status of being gay in the public eye in a boy band was enough to draw the ire of conservative factions of Irish society.

While facing resistance to their very existence at home, 4Guyz entered a pop music circuit that brought them into contact with different celebrity spheres. The band made headlines in 1996 when they met Boy George, who had just come out through his autobiography the previous year, at London's Gay Pride festival. In an article titled 'Guyz lashed, by George!' journalist Aileen O'Reilly wrote that word about 4Guyz spread 'like wildfire after they appeared at Pride in front of 250,000 fans at Clapham Common' and that when 'George was asked to interview the band, he told their PR to f**k off and after a litany of bitchy comments, he pointed a finger at the boys and stormed off'.[19] Recounting the incident, Mark recalls Boy George approaching the band with a microphone, commenting that each of the band members looked well in their tops, to which Mark responded playfully, 'Do you think we should take them off?' Boy George replied, 'No, you're too skinny for me,' at which point another member chipped in, 'Well rather that than being fat.' Offended by the jibes, Boy George dropped the interview. Outside of backstage shade-throwing with Boy George, 4Guyz went on the European Pride circuit, where they met Spice Girl Geri Halliwell at the Christopher Street Day celebration for Berlin Pride and took part in a fashion show with Chaka Khan, where they walked out on a runway before she performed her hit 'I'm Every Woman'.

From their foundation and launch earlier in the year, 4Guyz reached dizzy heights in what would become their short pop career. The UK gay press were particularly taken by the novelty of a gay Irish boy band. As the London *Pride 1996* magazine commented, 'The Republic of Ireland continued in its remarkable way in a queer year that saw all gay boy band 4Guyz launched there.'[20] While Boyzone was representative of a new Ireland that was postmodern, liberal and open, 4Guyz was touted for demonstrating how Ireland was, at least in some aspects, internationally, becoming a liberal enclave and leader around gay rights.

Following their successful performances and tours across Europe, by November 4Guyz had developed the commercial imperative of a coherent pop group, with a performance set list, a growing number of original songs and a stage presence to carry them through an entire show. One setback had hit the band's line-up towards the end of the summer when John McGurke departed, citing personal reasons.[21] Despite this, auditions were held to find a member that would 'fit in with the other four'.[22] Following this, however, it was decided that four members in 4Guyz actually worked – so the boy band finally lived up to its name, figuratively and literally. In November the band returned to Dublin for their first full concert in The Temple Bar Music Centre, where, by this stage, they had begun to draw the interest of major record labels. The band's management got in touch with Mike Stevens, Take That's former musical director, who helped to prepare them for meetings with the labels. With Stevens' input and 'major funk injection', 4Guyz shot the video for their track 'You Should Be Dancing' – a Bee Gees cover – in The Temple Theatre off Dorset Street, with the video and single release scheduled for the end of the year.[23] London Records became interested in signing the band and 4Guyz were about to make it big – before it all came crashing down.

A number of issues had arisen by the time it came to signing the record deal, including how the band should be marketed. While Junior Larkin felt that 4Guyz should appeal more directly to a gay fanbase, as was his original intention, John Pickering was conscious of the mainstream potential with the band's ability to cross over, especially given the significant amount of coverage they had received in such a short space of time. At the same time, the band members began to clash over songs and songwriting, and these disagreements at both management and band level led to 4Guyz becoming, as it were, 0Guyz, as the boys went their separate ways. The news hit the Irish gay press in 1997 when *GCN* reported that the band had split: 'Karl Anderson and Keith Lee left the four piece for personal reasons.' The article went on to say that the split was a surprise considering the record-company negotiations and that further tours for the band had been booked.[24]

4Guyz is a significant reference point not only in queer Irish culture, but in Irish cultural life generally. The band was formed when the Irish pop industry was producing a significant number of acts, including Only Us, First Kiss, the Carter Twins, Xplicit, Fab, Una and Just Girls and more successful acts such as OTT, B*Witched and, of course, Boyzone. 4Guyz were manufactured at a time when being openly gay in a boy band was an incredibly brave act in an industry innately built against them and based on heteronormatively led fandoms. To stand amid the plethora of Irish pop acts as out-and-proud, unabashed and unashamed, was a stark indication of an emerging cultural consciousness around the queer community in Ireland.

While long-term success evaded 4Guyz, Zrazy, a prominent lesbian music duo, emerged onto the Irish music scene and went on to have significant success that endures to this day. Known for their fearless advocacy of LGBTQ and feminist issues, Zrazy's journey in music began during a time when addressing such themes was especially challenging, given opposition from Ireland's conservative right.[25] Their early work, such as their first video featuring a lesbian kiss, pushed boundaries and was banned by a broadcaster.[26] Despite these obstacles, Zrazy produced award-winning music, receiving accolades like the USA GLAMA award, the Outmusic Award and a Billboard International win. Their songs, including 'Watch Your House (Ooh Ah, Paul McGrath)', which achieved number-one status in Ireland, have been powerful vehicles for promoting queer visibility and advocating for social and political issues.

While the world of pop and boy bands might sit firmly in the realm of the entrepreneurial and the aspirational, of making money and achieving success, 4Guyz, while not achieving longevity and sustained long-term success as a boy band, attempted to right an industrial wrong in the music industry, where pop stars were afraid of coming out and bands were afraid to engage with their gay fandoms. George Michael would not come out until 1998, followed soon after by Boyzone's Stephen Gately in 1999, but even in those two instances, the circumstances around it were not on their terms. George Michael was forced to come out after being caught up in a sting operation by a policeman in California; much like Stephen Gately who was compelled to do so before it came out in the press. The treatment of LGBTQ identities by the pop industry and society embedded fear around being out and open as a pop star, and 4Guyz went some way towards confronting and challenging this, long before mainstream acceptance of gay members in boy bands, girl bands and the greater pop industry.

3

'Bent Politicians'

*Gay and Lesbian Candidates
in 1980s Electoral Politics*

It is 1985 and the race for the Dublin City Council (then Dublin Corporation) elections is beginning to gather significant momentum with the polling day on the horizon. As candidates from across the parties canvass in districts and boroughs across the city, a young gay man knocks door-to-door, supported by a team of gays and lesbians working tirelessly from campaign headquarters in his kitchen in Rathmines. This young gay man is Tonie Walsh.

Tonie knows he has no chance of winning in this election. But that's not the point. Tonie has other ideas. The tools available to gay people in the mid 1980s for speaking with the public are virtually non-existent, especially in a climate where gay sex between men is a criminal offence and violence against queer people is rampant. The stakes are high and this election campaign, Tonie hopes, will bring a gay person to people's doorsteps, increasing gay visibility and engendering conversations.

As he knocks on the door of one flat in Harold's Cross this evening in 1985, not knowing what reception he is going to get, an older woman opens it. Tonie introduces himself, hands her a flyer. She reads his literature, which proudly declares him a gay candidate, looks him up and down and says, 'Aren't there enough bent politicians in Leinster House without electing another one?' As Tonie's jaw drops to the floor, the woman starts to laugh, assuring him that she's joking, indulging him in a conversation for a few moments before going back to her day and letting Tonie move onto the next door.[1]

This illustrates the creative strategies deployed by ordinary gay people who did extraordinary things in a country that was innately working against them. Knowing that they would not get elected, gay and lesbian people poured time, energy and money into a cause that would bring them to people's doorsteps, where, at the very least, members of the electorate might be willing to indulge the LGBTQ cause for a few minutes. No other platform allowed this level of conversation at the time. This is the story of how the lesbian and gay community used electoral politics to not only show the value in the gay vote, but also change people's perceptions of lesbian and gay people.

Tonie's experience is a far cry from the current political situation in Ireland. The last few government formations have seen several lesbian and gay people rise through the ranks to senior posts, such as Katherine Zappone as Minister for Children in 2016, Leo Varadkar as Taoiseach in 2017 and Roderic O'Gorman in 2020 as Minister for Children, Equality, Disability, Integration and Youth, with others becoming senators, including Colm O'Gorman and Fintan Warfield. In 2011, John Lyons, Jerry Buttimer and Dominic Hannigan were the first openly gay TDs elected. The possibility for LGBTQ individuals of entering the political sphere is now very much attainable, with the proverbial pink-glass ceiling being well and truly smashed. However, the criminalisation, invisibility and inequality wrought by the structures of the State in the 1980s made contesting in electoral politics a brave decision for an LGBTQ person and one that brought with it grave risk and responsibility.

Fighting in the local and general elections throughout the 1980s was seen by the gay community as a means of setting the agenda for Ireland's sexual minorities. While there was no expectation that any of these candidates would ever win, standing for election ensured, at the very least, visibility for lesbian and gay issues. And while fielding LGBTQ candidates was important for visibility, it was also a crucial means of showing the importance of the gay, or lavender, vote. Gay and lesbian candidates reminded people that they were a legitimate voting population with legitimate concerns that were 'up for grabs' by parties and candidates.[2] So as well as being an important political strategy for keeping gay issues on the agenda, lesbian and gay participation in electoral politics was considered a force for empowering the gay vote.

The first openly gay candidate to run for election in Ireland was David Norris. Seeing an opportunity when the prominent politician Noël Browne won a seat in the

Dáil and freed up a Trinity senate seat, Norris decided to campaign for the vacated spot in 1977, seeing it as a 'marvellous way to propagandise some influential people who were the opinion formers in Irish society ... I also wanted to widen the discussion on gay rights.'[3] With the help of his campaign manager, Edmund Lynch, Norris's Seanad attempt began an uphill and difficult battle. His campaign began the same year that US politician and gay-rights activist Harvey Milk was elected to San Francisco's Board of Supervisors, where Milk was active on anti-gay discrimination.[4] Both Milk and Norris reflected the motivation to directly enter the political sphere to enact change for their respective communities, with both encountering endemic societal homophobia while doing so. Harvey Milk would later be assassinated in November 1978 by fellow San Francisco supervisor Dan White.[5]

Norris failed to win a seat in the 1977 election, achieving 220 first preferences, but he continued to stand and increased his share from 1981 through to 1983, until eventually winning in 1987.[6] That year Norris stated that he had been the subject of homophobic remarks and 'scores of predictable jokes about keeping one's back to the wall when "that bum boy" was about'.[7] While David Norris has become a recognisable global political figure within LGBTQ politics, the story of LGBTQ people harnessing the power of elections for the greater good of Irish gays and lesbians is far more expansive.

The 1981 and 1982 general elections saw Ireland's first openly LGBTQ candidate run, when lesbian Liz Noonan, one of the founding members of Liberation for Irish Lesbians (LIL), contested the Dublin South-East constituency.[8] Noonan's election posters proudly declared her a 'lesbian feminist', as she stood on a ticket that centred around not only her lesbian identity but also women's issues, in particular divorce, abortion, women's centres, contraception and the end of violence against women.[9] Noonan's lesbian feminist candidacy proved crucial in obtaining visibility in the national press in Ireland. One article during the 1981 election included an interview with a constituent who was amused by it: 'Ah well, it livens things up a bit. The fact is, we're sick of all the parties and candidates and it needs a bit of something different to keep any interest at all.'[10] Noonan's campaigning was relatively well-received by the press and constituency, and journalistic reportage also acknowledged a growing sensibility and awareness of the political potential of the gay vote when Frank McDonald wrote in *The Irish Times*, 'Liz Noonan, a lesbian feminist, should get the more militant gay vote.'[11] While McDonald's specific meaning regarding the militancy of the gay vote was unclear, the fielding of lesbian candidates like Noonan indicated the political potential and also the potential for visibility evident with LGBTQ candidates. Even though Noonan was unsuccessful, she did receive 309 first-preference votes, the highest of any independent candidate who ran in that constituency. Her candidacy highlighted a number of issues regarding lesbian and feminist causes to voters, while also illuminating the power of the gay vote – most importantly, perhaps, to the politicians she was running against. Dublin South-East was a political hotbed at the time, with many stalwarts of Irish politics emerging from the area, including the leader of one of Ireland's largest political parties and Taoiseach for much of the 1980s, Garret FitzGerald. Participation in electoral politics had the potential to platform gay issues for senior political figures, especially when out LGBTQ people made the private matter of their sexuality public in the political sphere, a radical gesture serving to progress the gay and lesbian cause.

The participation of lesbian and gay individuals in elections as candidates was not a frequent occurrence in the 1980s, but it did tend to make a splash when it happened. Following Liz Noonan, Tonie Walsh ran for the aforementioned Dublin Corporation elections of 1985, and while he only received 190 first-preference votes and was eventually eliminated, those near-couple-of-hundred votes showed what was possible in an attempt to court an urban gay vote. While individual candidates attempted to make their mark, lesbian and gay organisations similarly tried to politically mobilise the LGBTQ community. The National Gay Federation (NGF), for example, ran voter-registration campaigns for gays and lesbians, which provided information about the value of registering to vote and how the gay and lesbian community could use their vote to influence conversations around election time and put pressure on politicos.[12] Voter registration, then, was about making lesbians and gay men aware that, despite the limited options around them for amplifying their voices, the gay vote could be a way of rocking the system.

As the gay-rights movement became more confident and cohesive, the success of David Norris at the European Court of Human Rights in 1988, where the court ruled that Ireland's criminal laws around sex between men must be reformed, prompted a new group to emerge: the Gay and Lesbian Equality Network (GLEN). GLEN quickly became cognisant of the fact that the conversation around decriminalisation and implementing the reform of the criminal laws was of paramount importance. As a result, GLEN made the decision to leverage the 1989 general election as an opportunity for the gay community to promote gay rights and liberation and, most importantly, put pressure on the government to ensure that reform of the criminal law stayed on the agenda. To that end, three gay male candidates stood for election: Tonie Walsh, again in Dublin South-East, Pastor Michael Foley of the Metropolitan Community Church in Dublin South-Central, and Don Donnelly, against then sitting Taoiseach Charles Haughey, in Dublin North-Central. Quite impressively, Pastor Foley received 1,122 first preferences. The candidates ran on a five-plank platform, demanding the following legislation:

> An anti-discrimination law in housing, employ-
> ment and access to employment for lesbian and
> gay men, ethnic minorities and travelling people;

An end to discrimination in the area of custody rights and access to children for lesbian mothers and gay fathers;

A single age of consent for all;

Legislation to allow lesbians and gay men to bequeath pension and property rights to a nominate partner;

The introduction of compulsory sex education in Irish schools, which must include non-judgemental education on sexual diversity.[13]

Donnelly explicitly noted that the motivation for standing for election centred around the fact that 'there has been very little discussion in Parliament or in public about lesbian and gay issues. We hope that by fighting this election we will highlight what Irish people mean by gay rights.'[14]

Much like the participation of lesbian and gay candidates in previous elections, the GLEN candidates never expected to win, but they realised that they had to take a major stand regarding criminal reform and that this election was crucial for engendering conversations with the public as well as with political representatives. Significant alliances were established: Tonie Walsh noted how he struck up a working relationship with Green Party candidate John Gormley, who was running in his first election in 1989. (Gormley would subsequently go on to lead the Greens and enter a coalition government with Fianna Fáil in 2007, where he would be a major proponent of implementing the Civil Partnership Bill.)

Similarly, Tonie Walsh's election campaign brought him into the fray against Labour candidate Ruairí Quinn, and a lot of Tonie's votes were distributed to him following his elimination.[15] Ruairi Quinn would go on to become a member of the government in 1993, with a Fianna Fáil–Labour coalition where he was Minister for Enterprise and Employment. It was this government that would finally reform the criminal laws around gay sex with men. Having gay and lesbian candidates then brought the community and their issues directly into contact with key stakeholders and decision-makers in the State and, while electoral success evaded many of them, the true power of their candidacy lay in the fact that were able to exert influence. Standing for election helped to amplify their voices. Significantly, GLEN's fielding of political candidates in the general election helped them to develop a significant bank of contacts and connections in the political sphere, which they subsequently used to lobby the government over various issues during its operation.

Since then, many candidates have run for election, both as independent LGBTQ candidates campaigning for LGBTQ issues – such as Lisa Connell in the 2009 local elections for Dublin City Council – and as out LGBTQ candidates for political parties. Connell's manifesto included an introduction stating 'My name is Lisa Connell and I'm here to recruit you', drawing upon and alluding to her LGBTQ political forebears, as this line was used by Harvey Milk in his political materials.[16] Much like the Republic, Northern Ireland has witnessed the growing visibility of LGBTQ politicians. During the 2014 to 2019 council term, three openly gay politicians were elected to Belfast City Council, which included Jeffrey Dudgeon of the Ulster Unionist Party, Mary Ellen Campbell of Sinn Féin and Julie-Anne Corr of the Progressive Unionist Party.[17]

The story of ordinary lesbian and gay citizens standing for election in the 1980s represents a significant political strategy to get the community to realise the power of the lavender vote, as well as amplifying the voice of the community in a cultural environment where the options for communicating with the public on gay issues were minimal. Significantly, standing bravely in these elections in such an oppressive climate also resulted in interaction with the political world and senior figures within it. Establishing alliances there resulted in important collaborative endeavours and influence, which would pave the way for gay law reforms and additional LGBTQ legislation in the years that followed, and in some ways demonstrated the political capacity of the gay community in terms of engaging with the electorate and the power of their vote – something that was fully realised many years later during the marriage-equality campaign in 2015. The candidacies of Liz Noonan, Tonie Walsh, Don Donnelly and Pastor Michael Foley elevated individual lesbian and gay figures to a broader area of influence that, despite not achieving success in the voting booth, at the very least changed some minds on the canvassing trail and in the political sphere, one doorstep and conversation at a time.

4

'The Dowager Queen of the Transvestites'

*Judith Storm and Gender Diversity
in Late-Twentieth-Century Ireland*

During the 1950s, like many children, Judith Storm was sent down the country, away from her native Dublin, to give her parents a break but also to give Judith a sense of country life. Judith had been raised as a boy by her parents, but throughout her childhood had gravitated towards ideas of femininity, particularly around presenting herself publicly as a woman, especially through dress. During those long summer months, Judith spent a lot of time with her aunt. But when her aunt went out, Judith would use the time to explore the house and property until one day, when Judith was fifteen, she entered her cousin's bedroom – the young woman had just left home to live in the UK. On exploring her wardrobe, Judith became enamoured with the clothes within – the style, the fashion and, most crucially, the femininity they exhibited. Trawling

through the garments, Judith felt an urge to try something on and decided upon what would be her first
female outfit: her cousin's school uniform.

And so she did. This was a catalysing moment for
Judith, who began to regularly wear the school uniform,
walking around the house and getting a feel for this new
side to herself.[1] What made this discovery particularly
striking for her was that it clashed with how she had
been raised, as, up until that point, she had been assumed
to be and socialised as a boy. Discovering her cousin's
clothes revealed to Judith a world of femininity and an
opportunity to express a womanhood that was innately
within her. As she recalls, she realised that her female
persona was 'always there, and changing my clothes
[revealed who] I really was'.[2]

One day the inevitable happened, and her aunt
came home early to find Judith in her daughter's school
uniform. The older woman remained silent until dinner
time, when she turned to Judith and asked, 'What was
all of that about?' Judith tried to explain as best she
could how the clothes made her feel truly herself. To
her great surprise, she found that, while her aunt was
confused, she was sympathetic, and they agreed to
keep it between themselves. In what was an Ireland of
very strict gender norms, in the 1950s – particularly
in the context of the Roman Catholic Church – her
aunt's acceptance of gender diversity was revolutionary
for Judith. She let Judith wear her daughter's clothes
for the rest of the summer, even buying new ones as
Judith began to find her own style. Judith's aunt felt she

had gained a daughter and even taught Judith how to cook and sew. This social transition and exploration of Judith's gender identity lasted for a number years until her aunt departed for the States, ending 'Judith's youthful transvestite summers'.[3]

While Judith would later get married and have children, those early summers at her aunt's house, dressing and expressing herself as a woman, became a crucial part of her identity. The tools, space and generosity her aunt gave inspired Judith to offer that same generosity to others, through her activism and establishment of different groups around gender diversity.

Judith Storm, a self-identifying transvestite, was central to enabling and helping others experiencing some form of gender diversity in late-twentieth-century Ireland. Her story is one that navigates an ever-evolving community trying to find its footing along with yet outside of the lesbian and gay activism happening during this period. From establishing and participating in groups such as the Irish Transvestite Organisation, the National Transvestite Group and the National Transvestite Line, Judith was central in forging spaces, places and community for gender minorities, particularly during a time when trans and gender-minority identities were subjected to frequent media hysteria. While Judith's is just one story of trans activism amongst many, it is one that demonstrates how gender minorities in Ireland are not just a footnote in queer Irish history but were, in fact, revolutionary in their activism and central to developing an Irish trans culture.

From a contemporary perspective, 'transvestite' as a term has become outdated, with 'cross-dresser' often being used instead. A transvestite is generally defined as 'a person who wears clothing, accessories, jewellery or make-up not traditionally or stereotypically associated with their assigned sex'.[4] 'Transgender', on the other hand, emerged in the 1980s and 1990s as an umbrella term for a range of gender-variant identities and communities.[5] I use the term 'transvestite' here for a number of reasons. This was how Judith Storm identified, both in personal letters to other gender-non-conforming people and in public interviews. As Emmet Harsin Drager and Lucas Platero argue, both 'transvestite' and 'transsexual' are now considered outdated terms, but the 'forward march of transgender has buried the fact that there are many living people who still identify with and live under those signs'.[6] While thinking around gender identity and gender non-conformity has developed over time, Drager and Platero note that the 'terms transvestite, travesti, cross-dresser, and their various idiomatic iterations are too often understood as not fully actualized transgender' and stuck in a particular historical period.[7] To that end, to not acknowledge both transsexual and transvestite as identity categories risks the erasure of those who, throughout history, identified in this way.

The 1970s saw Judith emerge as a leader of sorts around the transvestite community in Ireland. Following her marriage and after she had had her children, she became more comfortable in her identity as a transvestite and decided to pick a name for herself, settling on Judith Storm: Storm deriving from a character in a book she had read as a child and Judith being a variation of her middle name.[8] As she started to engage with organisations dedicated to gender minorities in the UK, Judith aimed to establish some sort of movement on the island of Ireland.

She began to engage with the Beaumont Society in 1970 and became its Irish representative with the intentions of establishing an Irish chapter. The Beaumont Society was a London-based organisation established in 1965 as a support group for male-to-female cross-dressers, and serving as an offshoot of US transgender activist Virginia Prince's Foundation for Full Personality Expression.[9] Yet from the outset, Judith had reservations around the policing of sexual identity within the Beaumont Society – the group only allowed heterosexuals. In light of this, Cara-Friend, a gay organisation in Belfast approached her in 1978 about setting up a group catering to 'transvestites of all shades of sexuality'.[10] This resulted in the foundation of the Irish Transvestite Organisation, which Judith described as a 'loose confederacy of transvestites whose sole unifying trait is their transvestism'.[11] A Belfast-based gay-rights group provided a meeting space for transvestites to attend monthly meetings, with around thirty to forty people attending every month. In a letter to *The Female Impersonator*, a US-based magazine for transvestites and burgeoning drag queens with a global readership, Judith explained how she was only comfortable dressing and expressing herself in Belfast, since Dublin felt a little too close to home for her at that point – Belfast provided her some anonymity.[12] But even Belfast presented a number of issues for transvestites, particularly in the context of the Troubles, with 'travelling en femme a risky business' (members of the IRA would often dress as women to avoid searches at checkpoints).[13]

Despite the Troubles, Judith carved out a space for socialisation in Northern Ireland, but noted how this was significantly more difficult in the Republic, where she observed that transvestites were far more fearful about being seen.[14] This was especially challenging in a cultural context where the media refused to acknowledge any kind of gender non-conformity at best, and generated hysteria around gender minorities at worst. Judith tried to place adverts in an attempt to establish the Irish Transvestite Organisation more prominently in Dublin, yet on only two occasions was an advert printed; the third time it was rejected by the advertising manager. 'I wrote to the advertising manager and explained the non-sexual side of things but he would not budge. If you are blackballed by one paper, you are blackballed by them all,' Judith noted.[15] While advertisers were refusing to give space to support groups, column inches were simultaneously dedicated to disparaging gender minorities like transvestites. An *Irish Independent* article from 1979 reported on a furore around the appearance of a transvestite on RTÉ's *The Late Late Show*, noting that 'a transvestite should not have been allowed to go on and certainly not have been allowed to advertise on RTÉ for young boys with similar urges to join his club'.[16]

The *Sunday World* in particular, throughout the 1980s, was a purveyor of hysterical articles generating shame, stigma and fear around transvestites, with headlines such as 'That's No Lady, That's My Husband' and 'The Highly Secret World of Ireland's Transvestites'.[17]

Despite these significant obstacles, Judith managed to create a community through various transvestite befriending groups throughout the 1970s and into the 1980s. She took part in the newly founded Friends of Eon group, which was established in 1978 by Claire Farrell and a person known as Lola. The group was named after Eon, a seventeenth-century French spy who gained access to a Russian court because he was dressed as a woman.[18] The Friends of Eon started from small meet-ups of transvestites, but grew to welcome a broader spectrum of gender minorities outside of cross-dressers. Claire and Lola secured a space in a disused room of the Parliament Inn (now the Turk's Head) and placed an advert in *In Dublin* magazine, suggesting guests 'come dressed as you like'.[19] The Friends of Eon would continue in various formations over the course of twenty years.[20]

As Judith moved in and around trans organisations and transvestite groups, she formalised her politics by joining the NGF, where she was elected to the administrative council in January 1988. During her time in the NGF, which was then based in Dublin's Hirschfeld Centre, Judith started a transvestite group – 'every Wednesday from 8.00–10.00 and is open to all transvestites irrespective of their sexual preference'.[21] Known as the National Transvestite Group, its aim was to give advice on clothes and make-up and any other help one might need. Outside of group meet-ups, Judith also offered a counselling service and one-on-one chats with anyone who wanted it.[22] One volunteer with the group recalled how Judith and the volunteers used to go shopping for clothes and make-up with people who came in to use the service. They would go to shops such as Brown Thomas or Dunnes Stores and pretend they were shopping for a mother or sister, giving sizes purporting to be for their family member but in actual fact for the person that wanted to express themselves as the opposite gender. The volunteer would accompany the individual, helping them find the right make-up and clothes size, often pretending to also be a family member – whatever helped someone to find their style and make them feel comfortable.[23] While the group was designated a transvestite group, Judith accommodated anyone from a gender minority who came looking for answers to questions, help or community.

Judith also sought to ensure that the National Transvestite Group had a national reach by attempting to establish a presence in Cork. While working on the National Transvestite Line, Judith said, 'we are amazed at the number of calls we are getting from outside of the immediate Dublin metropolitan area. A number of these have come from Cork (city and county), Limerick, Kerry and Waterford.'[24] She observed that many individuals outside Dublin who needed a space to express their gender identity could not do so on a routine basis by travelling to the capital. To Judith, it was essential that anyone, from anywhere across the country, should have access to somewhere local they could express themselves.

What is particularly striking about Judith's approach to gender politics was the way in which she attempted to educate about gender identity. She primarily used media platforms within the gay community, such as *GCN*, and national newspapers to expand how people engaged with ideas of gender and to educate on transvestism, pointing out the ambiguity of the term and how it's often misconstrued as fetishistic or pathological due to 'pseudo-scientific claptrap'.[25] She aimed to educate both the LGBTQ community and the broader public about gender variance, advocating that gender is more than just male or female, but rather a spectrum where individuals stand at different points. She stressed the distinction between sexual and gender identities, emphasising that they aren't automatically linked.[26]

Beyond her forward thinking around gender politics, the National Transvestite Line proved to be one of Judith's most significant social enterprises, helping not only an inordinate amount of people who identified as transvestites, but also the broader trans community, along with their families. By the early 1980s, many of the transgender and transvestite befriending groups across the city were becoming inundated with queries, so a resource where all of these questions and counselling services could be channelled would be significantly helpful. In 1983, Judith decided to lead the way by setting up a phone line.[27] Many of the early calls were from people Judith referred to as 'transvestites in the closet' – some of whom were contemplating suicide, unable to work out whether they were gay or not.[28] Much of the work Judith performed on the phone lines was to explain the differences between gender and sexual identity while destigmatising transvestism. This was particularly gruelling since, she explained, 'There are many confused, scared and hurt people out there in remote Irish villages, some of them deserted by their wives, who just can't come to terms with their transvestism.'[29] On one occasion a fully dressed cross-dresser rang Judith in a distressed state from a public telephone box, observing a group of teenagers in her path. Over the course of several minutes Judith calmed her down, telling her to 'just walk past them like any other woman and don't look them in the eye'.[30]

Judith also offered many callers practical advice 'on which Dublin shops were sympathetic to [transvestite] requirements' and which pubs and clubs on the gay scene allowed dressing services in their venues. Shops, restaurants and businesses were given the opportunity to be listed as transvestite-friendly by registering with the helpline. Judith regularly recommended Dunnes Stores for clothes shopping, as the sales people were 'well used to men coming up to buy articles of women's clothing. You can just say you're buying for your wife, she's about your size, and you'll have no problem.'[31] Strikingly, the wives of transvestites made up a significant part of the caller base, with many of them asking, 'Is my husband gay' or 'Is my husband going to leave me for another woman?'[32] Judith would explain cross-dressing and transvestism, noting that it was a form of gender expression, often leading to more understanding and a sense of relief for the spouses. While the vast majority of families and wives were receptive, the National Transvestite Line did receive accusations of spreading immorality and being 'responsible for husbands being transvestites'.[33] The national reach of her work with the helpline brought Judith much media attention, and she regularly appeared on local radio throughout the country. On one appearance on Louth radio station LMFM, an older woman rang up the studio to praise Judith, inviting her to her house up the road for lunch.[34]

Yet there was a lot of uncertainty regarding transvestites and the trans community and their relationship with the law. While cross-dressing was not illegal, gender minorities could potentially fall victim to an unsympathetic garda, who might consider their cross-dressing as 'conduct likely to lead to a breach of the peace' and 'conduct likely to insult a female'.[35] This became all too real for Judith on one occasion when her handbag was stolen as she walked through St Stephen's Green. While she attempted to chase the muggers with her skirt hitched up, she eventually had to give up and go into the Gaiety Theatre to call the gardaí. At that point, Judith felt some reticence. While the gardaí had been sympathetic while Judith gave her report, when they asked for her name she realised that the sympathy could dissipate very quickly. She eventually asked what name they wanted, to which the reply was, 'Whichever name you are most comfortable with.'[36]

Fear of discrimination was also an issue within the broader LGBTQ community. For instance, The George pub at one point banned transvestites on the basis of a policy of not 'allowing cross-dressers' – despite the fact that the same venue allowed drag shows on its main stage most nights of the week.[37] The George's policy subsequently was overhauled with a management changeover. Judith used her platform to expose the forms of gender policing that occurred both within and outside of the community in media columns and articles, attempting to make social institutions and gay and lesbian spaces more inclusive of gender minorities.[38]

By the 1990s and into the 2000s Judith Storm had been dubbed by an unnamed member of the Irish government as 'the dowager queen of the transvestites'.[39] Whether given in jest, admiration or as an insult, Judith wore the title with pride. She was a proponent of demonstrating how sex and gender diversity were part of human nature and she provided a transitionary space for so many of Dublin and greater Ireland's transvestites and gender minorities to express who they truly were. The roots of today's trans activism can be traced back to trans activists such as Judith Storm, along with Claire and Lola from the Friends of Eon. Judith outrightly confronted discrimination on the basis of gender identity and gender expression, as she worked to reduce prejudice and ensure that the community's specific needs were provided for. Judith Storm, most crucially, was at the vanguard of that early wave of gender politics and trans activism during the burgeoning days of queer Irish culture, demonstrating that trans people have always been part of our history.

5

A Private Matter?

Gay Soldiers in the Irish Army

On a cold day in March 1977, P.J. Brennan said goodbye to his family in Clonmel and got into a Land Rover that was to take him to his new home for the foreseeable future – the Curragh Camp in Kildare. What P.J. was driving towards, as the wind and the rain relentlessly beat down on the vehicle, was a new career in the Irish Defence Forces as a recruit in the latest platoon of the Irish Army.

On arriving to the Curragh Camp, somewhat startled after the long drive, P.J. found himself surrounded by red-brick buildings at the General Training Depot. He was quickly given his kit and shown to his billet, which he would share with other seventeen-year-old men from around the country. Later that night, having settled into his new environment with some trepidation, he went to the canteen and found some familiar faces from his billet. One of them stood out to him: immediately, and for reasons unknown to him, P.J. felt a connection.

As the evening progressed, each of the new recruits gradually retired for the night, eventually leaving P.J. with his new friend. Once they were alone together P.J. realised that he was very attracted to this man and, after some more drinks, it became clear that the attraction was mutual. And so that night P.J. and his comrade shared a romantic and sexual encounter, beginning a relationship of sorts for their duration as recruits. By day both men were engaged in intense training, which might include 'jogging at seven in the morning across the plains of the Curragh and leaving holes six inches deep in the snow and muck. Nothing to see for miles around but SSS (better known as sheep, shite and soldiers).'[1] At night and anytime there were gaps in their regimented training schedule, both would find time to be together away from the prying eyes of other soldiers and the military police, in turf stores and even, on one occasion, on the empty rifle range.

Despite developing this significant romantic connection, P.J. and his lover were all too aware of the dangers of being gay in the army. As P.J. remembers, every day 'all sorts of nasty comments were passed' and a 'few so-called suspects were pointed out'; being considered not 'typical army material', their lives were subsequently made miserable.[2] While P.J. and his lover eventually went their separate ways, their relationship could have exposed them to endemic abuse within the Irish Army at that time and resulted in them being discharged: in 1977 the Irish State still prohibited homosexual acts. Furthermore, any offence under criminal law was also an offence under military law under the Defence Act 1954. A climate of criminality crept into the Irish Defence Forces, creating an oppressive atmosphere for many of the gay men who joined, seeking to give service to their country, before decriminalisation in 1993. David Norris recalls being involved in a case as a leader within the gay-rights movement where one gay soldier 'got a very bad beating and lost an eye, but I was not able to continue with the case as the family did not want the publicity'.[3] While in the ancient world, homosexuality in the military was regarded as contributing towards morale, especially amongst the Spartans in Ancient Greece, the army in late-twentieth-century Ireland took a more restrictive and policed view on gay people.

One man who wanted to serve his country was Tom Brace, who at the age of sixteen joined An Fórsa Cosanta Áitiúil (FCA), the army reserve, a part-time component of the Defence Forces comprising volunteers participating in army training in their spare time. During his time as part of the 20th Infantry Battalion in the FCA, Tom became attracted to another man in the unit, which was reciprocated. 'We would go out on the range in a truck and sit and put our arms around each other. It was all supposed to be camaraderie, but I knew he was attracted to me and I was crazy about him but it never developed into a relationship in that sense,' he explains.[4]

Tom decided to join the Permanent Defence Forces in 1968, fully committing himself to a career with the Irish Army. At the back of his mind, however, was the knowledge that he was attracted to men. and he knew that 'this would not be tolerated officially'.[5] On entering the army full-time to start his training on the Curragh, Tom had to make the decision to keep his sexuality under wraps: 'I reckoned I had the discipline to keep it under control. That was my aim.'[6] The stakes were high. He knew that, on the one hand, homosexual acts between men were a criminal offence in the State and under military law. On the other hand, he knew that, in practice, if homosexuality was 'detected' in any way by senior members of the army's command, 'You were given twenty-four hours' notice and you were discharged, officially referred to by the Defence Forces as "services no longer required", where soldiers would just simply be thrown out onto the street.'[7] While the reasoning behind the discharge was often not officially recorded by the Defence Forces, the victims could opt for an appeal, but this would result in their discharge becoming part of a court-martial – a mechanism for the enforcement of military law and, as a result, leading to a soldier's gay identity becoming public.

In light of all this, Tom knew he had to be careful. 'I walked a narrow path and I stayed on the straight and narrow. I had to. I was terrified of being found out. There was conflict between my sexual desire and my career and I wanted to stay in the army,' he recalls. Tom began to find it increasingly difficult to conceal his sexuality while managing what was becoming a stellar career as he rose through the Defence Forces ranks. He received the prize for best soldier on his platoon in the 3rd Infantry Battalion, which secured him a place on a Non-Commissioned Officer (NCO) course, leading to his promotion to Sergeant. Over the course of his twenty-one-year career, Tom also completed four overseas tours, with one of his most significant achievements being the year he spent as Company Sergeant in the humanitarian branch of the United Nations (UN) headquarters in Nicosia as part of the UN's peacekeeping force in Cyprus. Military law also applied overseas, so any kind of overt expression of his sexuality was completely forbidden. However, his UN colleagues from Sweden, the Netherlands and Belgium were more liberal than their Irish counterparts. This was because gay people could openly serve in those countries since the mid 1970s. So he found some brief moments with those colleagues in the UN to share who he truly was, albeit quietly and discreetly.

Religion also deterred Tom's expression of his sexuality, and he recalls the army chaplain having a great deal of influence on the army's leadership. If anyone was in trouble, for example, they could ask the chaplain to vouch for them and potentially prevent them from getting court-martialled. One specific aspect of service in the army that made clear the Catholic influence hanging over Tom and his fellow soldiers was the compulsory church parade, which involved units marching as a group towards an army barracks' local church. While soldiers were not forced into the church, they had to wait outside until the mass had finished.

Over the course of his career, Tom came across other soldiers in similar situations – yet none of them ever acted on their desire because they wanted to ensure that they kept their livelihoods. This commitment to the army highlighted the unique challenges faced by soldiers who, due to their deep identification with the Defence Forces, struggled to envision an alternative civilian life where they could live as openly gay. For them, transitioning out of the DF meant not just changing jobs, but also losing their identity, social connections, occupation and home. Meanwhile, Tom continued to rise up the ranks, transferring to the military police and later to the 20th Infantry Battalion as a training NCO in the Pearse unit, where he was later promoted to a Company Quartermaster Sergeant (CQMS). At a point, a small number of senior members became aware of his sexuality but kept it under wraps and advised Tom to be very careful: while the broader cultural climate of the Defence Forces was oppressive, sympathetic allies were to be found in some places, and they made all the difference.

Tom was discharged from the Eastern Command of the Defence Forces after twenty-one years of service on 6 November 1989, his certificate of discharge noting his exemplary military conduct. During his service, the Defence Forces had given Tom the opportunity to complete his Leaving Certificate, as he had left school early to work and provide for his family. Tom achieved excellent results, which earned him a place at Trinity College Dublin for a degree in English and History, which he took up following his career in the military. Yet, although Tom dabbled in Dublin's expanding gay scene – going to The George a few times, for example – he did not fully immerse himself in gay culture while he was in the army. The price was simply too high for him. 'I left school at fifteen, I was a factory labourer and I didn't want to go back to that. If I had been discharged, I would have been looking for a job as a labourer and I knew I wasn't going to get married,' he says.[8] In light of this, Tom avoided focusing on the price he paid for his career in terms of being who he truly was as a gay man. Despite these immense difficulties, he was very proud to serve his country and have the career that he did with the Irish Army.

However, there was to be a strange twist of fate on one of his first English courses, when he signed up for a seminar on James Joyce. Dutifully attending his tutorial, along with his copies of *Dubliners* and *A Portrait of the Artist as a Young Man*, he excitedly waited for the tutor to arrive and engage in all things Joycean. As the door opened and the tutor walked in, Tom realised that it was none other than David Norris, one of the pioneers of gay civil rights in Ireland. The gay community was one that Tom felt he could never truly be a part of. And yet here, right in front him, was one of the most visible leaders of that movement. Over the next few weeks, as they explored the complex depths of Joyce's work, Tom tried to build up the courage to tell David that he was gay – something he still struggled with after years of keeping this part of himself under wraps – until one day he went up to David after class, took a deep breath and nervously said, 'David, I'm gay.' 'Good for you!' David bellowed happily in response. And from that interaction began a lasting friendship, where Tom could truly be himself.

While the army has historically been a difficult place to be gay, it has also had a contentious relationship with gender, particularly around the inclusion of women. The history of women's participation in the Irish Defence Forces has seen significant changes over the years. Up until 1979, women were explicitly barred from joining the army, Air Corps and Naval Service.[9] The shift began in 1980 when the first four female cadets entered the cadet school under the banner of the short-lived Women's Service Corps. By the end of that year, a total of eleven women had joined the ranks. The Women's Corps met its end in 1981, marking the start of the integration of women into the army. Yet, although no longer confined to a separate unit, female recruits were still excluded from combatant roles until 1992 when – following internal and external pressures – women achieved full integration, which included allowing them to enter combatant roles.[10] This milestone allowed them to perform identical duties, undergo the same training and serve in combat roles overseas, just like their male counterparts. Subsequently, women were granted entry into the Air Corps in 1990 and the Naval Service in 1995. Despite these advancements, women in the Defence Forces continue to grapple with a hostile environment marked by toxic masculinity and misogyny. This became evident in 2021 when a group of women who had experienced a culture of misogyny and sexual assault in the Defence Forces came together to form the Women of Honour, after an audio documentary of the same name that was broadcast recounting their experiences. The group subsequently put pressure on the Department of Defence to review the culture of bullying and abuse in the Defence Forces, with an initial report being produced in March 2023.[11]

The criminal law reform and debates around the decriminalisation of homosexuality in 1993 raised a number of questions for the Irish Defence Forces, compelling the Irish Army to acknowledge the issue on a public level for the first time. The situation around gays in the US military also generated conversation around the issue in the Irish Army in early 1993. New US President Bill Clinton had just made a policy proposal that was creating a significant amount of conflict between the White House, military leaders and congress. As a presidential candidate, Clinton had pledged support to eliminate the US Defence Department's ban on gay troops and, on entering office, immediately encountered resistance from military leaders who felt that their 'commands would be devastated if homosexuals are allowed to trumpet their sexual preferences'.[12] Colin Powell, the Chairman of the Joint Chiefs of Staff (the highest military position in the US Defence Department), warned that 'the American military would be emasculated by resignations and conflict' if openly gay people were allowed to serve.[13]

A spokesperson from the Irish Army press office noted in response to Clinton's proposals that 'homosexuality is not unknown in the Irish Army' but that the question of sexuality should be a private matter and that 'a solider involved in a homosexual act would be tried under military law'.[14] In response, David Norris observed that the gay people 'who choose to join the army make good soldiers ... why are all these poor heterosexual men so frightened?'[15] *The Irish Times* commented that, in the wake of Clinton in the US, a code of conduct around interpersonal relations could be introduced to the Irish Defence Forces if decriminalisation of homosexuality were to occur.[16] Clinton would later have to compromise on a complete lifting of the ban on gay people in the military, and in its place 'Don't ask, don't tell' became the official policy in December 1993, whereby military personnel were prohibited from discriminating against or harassing closeted gay, lesbian or bisexual service members. Conversely, the act also prohibited gay, lesbian or bisexual service members from disclosing their sexual orientation.

In June of the same year, the Criminal Law Amendment Bill passed in Ireland, decriminalising homosexuality throughout the State and within the army and the navy. Military law now had to follow the law of the State.[17] Journalist Mary Kenny of *The Irish Independent* supported the change in legislation, stating through a somewhat strange juxtaposition, 'better a brave pansy than a cowardly straight'.[18] One of the critiques from more conservative parts of the Defence Forces and Irish society was that the law reform did not provide the army with a 'statutory opt out clause' for them to not 'recruit homosexuals'.[19] However, the army's position on gay relationships within the military was tested later in December 1993, when a relationship between two members of the Army School of Music was subjected to a court-martial and became front-page news in the *Evening Herald* and was reported elsewhere in the media.[20] The court-martial was the result of 'homosexual activities' between a senior NCO and a junior bandsman, and the charge was brought under Section 168 of the Defence Act.[21] The premise of the case, according to the Defence Forces, was not that it was a gay issue, but that the case breached the army's code around senior ranks not having relations with junior ranking members from the same unit.[22] In light of this, the staff association – the Permanent Defence Forces Representative Association – called on Minister for Defence David Andrews to accelerate a code of conduct around homosexuality and provide assurances that private relationships outside of the army barracks were not a source of interest for the military police.[23]

One first-hand witness to the army's period of transition around decriminalising homosexuality was Will Kennedy from Cork City, who joined in 1988. After a brief stint in a seminary, Will was trying to decide what he wanted to do with his life while also struggling with his gay identity – the army served as a vehicle of acceptance: 'I was trying to prove to everybody that I was a real man,' he explains. Will joined recruit training at Collins Barracks in Cork. On his first night, he recalls coming out of the shower and going into the billet he was sharing with ten other recruits when he heard someone say, 'Be careful, lads, this guy will stick a tail in you.'[24] This climate of homophobia was something that Will would have to contend with over the course of his career. People ended up being particularly hard on Will during recruit training, but it also made him 'more determined to do things twice, if not three times, as hard as everybody else'.[25]

Despite these initial obstacles, Will eventually successfully passed out with his platoon and applied for a three-year chef training course. For the next few years, aware of the implications of being openly gay in the army, he, for the most part 'kept his mouth shut and didn't do anything'. When he had go to the Glen of Imaal in Wicklow, military lands where army training took place, he would disappear during recreational evenings to drive into Dublin to gay bars, before returning to base early the next morning. However, with the change in the law in 1993, the pressure was no longer the same, and by 1994 Will decided to stop all the lies about his life and come out of the closet. As Will notes himself, gossip among men in the army spreads like wildfire, so he told only one or two of his comrades and word quickly flew around the barracks. He recalls that there was a lot of support from some people, but others in the barracks 'would walk to the other side [of the room] if they saw me coming'.[26] Despite the fact that Will could not be formally discharged for his sexual identity, the culture of the army was still oppressive. He would often get what he referred to as 'slagging' around his sexuality, which meant he had to defend himself and give as good as he got. Each day, he notes, 'I would have to put on a suit of armour, preparing my lines for any kind of insult that could come my way ... if you complained about it, it would only get worse.'[27]

Moments of support were notable, particularly on Will's overseas mission to the UN in Ethiopia and Eritrea. Sent to Eritrea's capital Asmara on a peacekeeping mission, Will was aware of the precarious situation around his sexuality in his new base. Homosexuality has been a criminal offence in Eritrea since 1957, with imprisonment of up to three years, so a placement there for a gay man was potentially risky. Unsure how safe he was, Will asked his platoon to not say anything about his sexuality and received full support over the course of the trip. In the context of post-decriminalisation in the army, and despite these pockets of support, Will still describes the army as a lonely place for gay men. Despite that, Will concluded his career in 2011, completing over twenty years of service. On his departure, he was the only open and out gay man in Collins Barracks in Cork.

Despite their desire to serve their country, the experiences of Tom and Will, and many other gay men like them, before and after the decriminalisation of homosexuality, reflect the difficulties and constraints around a career in the Irish Defence Forces. While many people made sacrifices to serve their country in the first place, the stakes were higher for gay people, who often had to park their identities at the door of the army barracks and survive in a tough cultural climate. This has recently been acknowledged by the Report of the Commission on the Defence Forces in 2022, which concluded that the army was a 'very uncomfortable place for females and lower status males or minorities to work'.[28] Significant efforts have been made since to bring more diversity into the Irish Defence Forces. In 2015 Minister for Defence Simon Coveney announced the Defence Forces wanted more gay people to apply.[29] In 2016, following the successful 'yes' vote in the same-sex marriage referendum the previous year, gay staff were allowed to have their weddings on military bases, like their heterosexual counterparts.[30] In that same year, Defend With Pride was established in the Defence Forces, which would provide aid, information and guidance for LGBTQ personnel and allies. The establishment of this group was a significant step towards making the army a diverse and inclusive workplace. In 2018, the Defence Forces marched in Dublin Pride for the first time.

While much has changed in the last few decades, historically many gay people were treated as criminals and abused in the Irish Defence Forces. Protections and measures need to continue to be put in place so that any member of the LGBTQ community who wishes to serve their country can do so safely, confidently and with pride around who they are.

6

Pink Carnations and
Pink Triangles

*The Emergence of Pride in
Ireland (1974–1982)*

At the height of summer in June 1985, John Calnan took the brave step to call the Gay Information helpline in Cork. Having come to terms with his identity as a gay man, he was ready to step out of the closet and build a community for himself. Gay Information Cork, which was being run by the Cork Gay Collective at the time, encouraged John to come into the Quay Co-Op that week to attend a meeting. Once his initial nervousness had dissipated, and over the course of several meetings, John quickly made lifelong friends. Among the group that first evening were Cork gay-rights pioneer Arthur Leahy and his then partner Laurie Steele. As the meeting came to an end, Laurie and Arthur informed John that Gay Pride was happening in Dublin the following weekend and that he should join. He immediately said yes and, the next Saturday, found himself on the way to Dublin in Arthur's car, which was to lead the parade from the front through the capital city's main streets.

John had no sense of what a Pride parade involved, so he decided that he might walk around Dublin for the afternoon and watch it from the edges. Those best-laid plans were quickly overturned when Laurie picked up one pole of the Cork Gay Collective banner to start marching in the parade and, turning to John, pointed at the other pole and said, 'Well, I can't carry it on my own!' For a moment, John was unsure, uncertain and nervous. The sheer visibility of what he was about to do, holding a banner declaring himself gay as he walked through the streets of Ireland's capital city, seemed daunting. Despite these reservations, John picked up the Cork Gay Collective banner and walked with Laurie as representatives of the Cork gay community.

John Calnan's story is one that reflects so many people's first experience of Pride – nervousness, trepidation, fear, but also excitement, joy and fun.[1] It also reflects the ways in which Pride is a communal riposte to the idea that LGBT lives should be hidden, fearful and lived in shame. By holding the Cork Gay Collective banner in Dublin Pride 1985, John, Laurie and many before and after them rejected the oppression of growing up in an Ireland that demanded silence and invisibility around LGBTQ lives. Instead, they ended that silence, proudly declaring who they were on the main streets of Dublin.

Today, Pride has become one of the most significant events across Ireland, with Dublin Pride in particular regularly attracting 60,000–80,000 people each year – a far cry from the 50–100 people that marched in John

Calnan's first march.[2] The 2023 Dublin Pride parade drew significant attention in the media, with many outlets declaring it the fortieth anniversary of Dublin Pride. Much of this coverage was incorrect, ignoring Pride activities that had been happening in Ireland since 1974, erasing an entire history of early Pride movements. Pride emerged in the late twentieth century in Ireland as a form of protest, activism and celebration and continues to the present day, demonstrating how events such as Pride evolve in a gradual and incremental way.

The beginnings of Pride in Ireland can be traced directly back to a broader movement occurring internationally around gay and lesbian liberation, specifically the seminal Stonewall Riots in June 1969. The Stonewall uprising was one of the most significant events in the history of LGBTQ liberation and a catalyst for the modern fight for LGBTQ rights. The events began at the Stonewall Inn, on 53 Christopher Street in New York, which was part of a network of illegal gay clubs and after-hours bars run by the Mafia in New York's West Village and functioned as a private club to navigate around licensing laws relating to the sale of alcohol.[3] The police regularly raided the Stonewall – typically, the lights would be turned off, the customers would be lined up and identification cards would be checked. In many instances, those without ID cards, or dressed in full drag, were arrested.[4] These raids continued until finally the community had enough and began to fight back on 28 June 1969, with the riots continuing until 3 July in a series of sporadic protests around the Stonewall Inn.

While Stonewall was a watershed moment, it was the culmination of decades of LGBTQ activism and agitation, which included several instances of activist anger such as the 1961 Black Nite Brawl in Milwaukee and the 1966 Compton's Cafeteria Riot in San Francisco.[5] In the run-up to the first anniversary of the Stonewall Riots, activist groups, involved in the original riots and beyond, sought to commemorate the event in some way. At the time, Reminder Day Pickets were held annually from 1965 to 1969 on 4 July at Independence Hall in Philadelphia, where activist groups organised marches and protests to campaign for gay rights.[6] Following the Stonewall Riots, the organisers behind the Reminder Day Pickets suggested harnessing the momentum of Stonewall and focusing their energy on an annual demonstration commemorating the riots. In November 1969 the Eastern Regional Conference of Homophile Organizations (an amalgamation of various gay-rights groups on the US east coast) proposed that 'a demonstration be held annually on the last Saturday in June in New York City to commemorate the spontaneous demonstrations on Christopher Street and this demonstration be called Christopher Street Liberation Day'.[7] New York, Los Angeles and Chicago set about organising events for the last Saturday of June in 1970. In New York, the Christopher Street Liberation Day involved a march to Central Park, with the theme of the event being 'Gay Pride' as a counterpoint to prevailing attitudes of shame. The tradition of Pride emerged from the theme of that first successful Christopher Street Liberation Day, and, from June 1970, annual Pride traditions began to emerge in nascent LGBT civil rights movements globally, as a form of protest, politicisation and partying, serving to celebrate the gay community's wins and redouble efforts to advance gay liberation further.

In the early 1970s, the efforts to commemorate the Stonewall Riots quickly became a transnational movement through Pride, which took a variety of forms, from parades to parties and protests to proms. The globality of Pride, particularly as a form of protest, can be seen from collaborative activists' efforts, especially in Europe, one of which resulted in Ireland's very first Pride demonstration. In June 1974, the Norwegian gay organisation Det Norske Forbundet announced that their Pride celebration for that year (Gay Liberation Day) would be dedicated to highlighting the criminal laws around homosexuality in Ireland and the climate of homophobia engendered by the Catholic Church.[8] The protest took the form of a demonstration outside Oslo's British embassy, with placards declaring 'Stop the oppression of Irish homosexuals'.[9] Encouraged by their Norwegian counterparts, Irish gay and lesbian activists arranged the first-ever Pride demonstration on 27 June 1974, where they similarly picketed outside of the British embassy in Dublin and then marched on to the Department of Justice with placards stating 'Homosexuals are revolting'.[10] David Norris, one of the activists present at the first Gay Pride march, recalls how many on the streets of Dublin were horrified to see such an overt and public declaration of homosexuality. He recounts that the

46A bus nearly crashed into the railings of St Stephen's Green, so shocked was the bus driver. Another incident involved a lorry that had just been parked outside the department to deliver a new carpet for the Minister for Justice's office. As Norris recalls, 'One man got off the lorry and said, "Jaysus Mick, fucking queers!" Mick got out, took one look at us and said, "What about it? I don't give a bollocks, a picket is a fucking picket." He took up my placard and walked around with us for five minutes.'[11] While Ireland's first Pride march and demonstration was a small affair, involving only twelve activists, the Pride 1974 event demonstrated the power of Pride as a protest, a means of creating solidarity with allies and a vehicle through which public visibility could be achieved.

While Pride continued to grow into an annual, broader international movement, its development stalled in Ireland from the mid to late 1970s. This was mainly because a small number of activists within the broader Irish gay civil rights movement were focusing on establishing solid physical and social infrastructures for the movement. The first flush of activism evident with the founding of groups such as the Irish Gay Rights Movement (IGRM) in 1974 saw these organisations channel energy into developing social and cultural outlets for the community, with a focus on finding physical spaces. Alongside this, the late 1970s saw a concerted effort around campaigning for the decriminalisation of homosexuality, with David Norris, Bernard Keogh and Edmund Lynch founding the Campaign for Homosexual

Law Reform in 1977. Notwithstanding this flurry of politicisation, a couple of these early groups imploded and fell apart. It would be five years before Pride would reemerge, in 1979, with the founding of a new organisation, the National Gay Federation (NGF). The NGF brought with it a fresh political and social structure, along with a more permanent physical space in the form of the Hirschfeld Centre, which provided the human and economic resources to realise a full Pride programme once again.

Ireland's first Gay Pride Week was organised for the final week of June 1979, with the NGF determined to ensure that the Stonewall Riots were commemorated. Gay Pride Week 1979 provided a suite of social, cultural and political activities, which demonstrated a growing movement and confidence within Irish gay civil rights activism. In terms of a political consciousness, a forum was held at the Hirschfeld Centre with members of Ireland's prominent political parties, including Michael Keating of Fine Gael, Niall Andrews of Fianna Fáil, Ruairi Quinn of the Labour Party and Noël Browne.[12] Political activities also took place on the streets, where a leafleting campaign was organised at the top of Grafton Street, engaging the public, asking them to support 'our campaign for legal and social change and explaining our views of life and what we see as our rights'.[13] In terms of cultural activities, Rainer Werner Fassbinder's movie about a gay man in West Germany who wins the lotto, *Fox and His Friends* (1975), was shown in the Hirschfeld's film theatre, the Hirschfeld Biograph, demonstrating an engagement with queer cultural production.[14] The Gay Pride Day event, which took place on the Sunday, was demarcated for a Pride Picnic, a tradition that would build and continue throughout the early 1980s. The picnic took place in the Hollow in the Phoenix Park, where attendees were told to 'bring along a musical instrument and wear a Gay Pride Week badge'.[15] The successful week of events started the momentum for a more consistent slate of events for Pride Week, coalescing simultaneously around a community growing in confidence and visibility and becoming more coherent in their political, social and cultural activities.

Gay Pride Week 1980 took place once again at the end of June, with the goal of reassuring gay and lesbian people that there was a community for them if they wished to join. Pride also continued to demonstrate to isolated LGBTQ people an awareness of shared existences and desires. The information leaflets developed by the NGF for Gay Pride 1980 explicitly connected the ideas of Pride with the Stonewall Riots, providing a brief history of the latter and how they generated a global Pride movement.[16] Tonie Walsh, one of the core organisers of Gay Pride 1980, noted how the distribution of leaflets and pink carnations was one of the cornerstones of Pride, enabling the community to directly engage with the Irish public. He recalls early on the Saturday morning of Gay Pride Week going down to the Smithfield flower market and buying boxes upon boxes of pink carnations to hand out alongside the information leaflets.[17] The pink carnation was a reference to gay Irish man and playwright Oscar

Wilde, who in 1892 'instructed a handful of his friends to wear [green carnations] on their lapels to the opening night of his comedy *Lady Windermere's Fan*'.[18] The green carnation became a subtle, subversive code around gay desire. Walsh notes that dyeing the many pink carnations green would just not have been possible at the scale necessary, but at the very least, using the carnations harnessed the cultural symbol of Wilde, venerating it through a Pride event.

Many members of the public were amused by young gay men and women walking around the streets, offering them pink carnations, and accepted leaflets about riots in New York they had never heard of. The leaflets stated: 'Stonewall is now eleven years past. The main assertions have been made, the necessity of being visible, to come out and let other people know you are gay. The other assertion was the need for community to come out together, to gain strength by everyone working together.'[19] Three calls for change were made within the leaflet: 'The right to form loving relationships without being labelled criminals, the right to live as citizens equal before the law and demand for education which suits our needs.'[20] For the most part, as Walsh recalls, the Irish public were good-natured about the traffic-stopping on the streets, accepting the pink carnations and putting them in their lapels. One Christian fundamentalist who was preaching beside St Stephen's Green took issue with the group and refused to take a carnation Robert Stephenson offered to him, denouncing the gay and lesbian community from his microphone. Eamon Somers, who was amongst the leaflet distributors that day, recalls initially feeling nervous, but found being visible on the streets, handing out this information, liberating.[21] The gay picnic was the culmination of the Pride Week once again, this year involving the release of two thousand pink balloons from St Stephen's Green. The picnic was especially important because, while it was primarily a social event, it also involved the reclaiming of a public realm that was traditionally hostile and unwelcoming. The picnic was organised to be convivial, public and visible, without inviting the glare of homophobia or potential violent attacks.

One of the more confrontational aspects of the early Pride events was the 'pub zap', a form of activist agitation that involved gays and lesbians, sporting apparel that identified them as LGBT, going into a pub and seeing how long it took until they were asked to leave the premises. The origins of the 'pub zap' can be traced back to a lesbian couple who decided to go for a drink in the Sackville Lounge behind Clerys department store in Dublin. The barman quickly noticed that they were a couple and threw them out. The women went back to the lesbian community and, upset and furious, reported the issue. A lesbian activist at the time, Murf, recalls how, 'It wouldn't have been the first time that gay and lesbian people had been asked to leave a pub,' so the group decided to go around local pubs from Dame Street to George's Street and see how bar management and staff would react.[22] The zap then became a significant part of the Pride programme of events, with the NGF referring to them as forcing 'people to think about the gay issue but suffer rejection as a result. In that sense, these annual booze-ups are ideally named zaps.'[23] In remembering her first Pride, Murf notes that there was no rainbow Pride flag that would have identified a group going to a bar as overtly gay – they wore pink triangles and badges declaring their sexuality.[24] On entering the bar, the group would see if they could get served from the counter, putting their arms around each other or holding hands. These experimental performative acts were deployed to establish where the safe spaces were across the city. During Pride Week 1982 the group were refused entry at the Clarence Hotel, and in the Lord Edward bar, they found themselves being threatened by gardaí because they were wearing pink triangles.[25] Murf especially notes the meaning of Pride for her on those early days of the pub zaps: 'Pride really was a protest and looking for recognition. It was our way of saying we are women who are gay. We are alive. We are well. We are not afraid to put our head up. Along with that, we would hope that anybody who saw would say, oh, there's a bunch of gay women, this is okay.'[26]

The Pride flag today has become the representational shorthand through which the community declares Pride month and celebrations. It was designed by Gilbert Baker at the request of Harvey Milk, who tasked him with creating an icon to symbolise the LGBT movement. Before the contemporary Pride flag became popularised, however, the early Pride movements in Ireland utilised the pink triangle, as Murf described, to indicate their identity as gay or lesbian.

The pink triangle's significance goes back to Adolf Hitler's Third Reich, where the Nazis cracked down on expressions of gender and sexuality that did not conform to their idea of 'Aryan race'. Gay men especially were not seen as part of Nazi plans for a 'new Germany', with a national law passed criminalising 'unnatural decency between men'. Between seven thousand and ten thousand gay men were sent to concentration camps, where their uniform was marked with a pink triangle.[27] In the 1970s, gay activists in West Berlin chose the pink triangle as a symbol that would 'signify the coming out of individuals and a social movement for gay rights', with activists wanting to turn this symbol of oppression into one of liberation. The Irish gay civil rights movement was aware of their queer European forebears and in much of their literature, activism and Pride activities fostered the pink triangle as the symbol of their identity, connecting two national communities and forming the basis of a shared gay history, while also commemorating those gay men who were murdered in Hitler's concentration camps. As Tonie Walsh notes, 'Our use of the pink triangle was not only to reference our European history and reinstate that history, but to also resist the monolithic cultural hegemony of the US.'[28]

Pride as a movement was not just a Dublin-centric enterprise but began to emerge as an annual event across the country. In 1981, as Patrick McDonagh notes, the Cork IGRM and Cork Gay Collective worked together to organise the first Gay Pride Week celebrations in Cork, although the Pride that year was a collaborative effort with Waterford, serving as a Munster Gay Pride of sorts.[29] One of the participants in and organisers of that first Gay Pride Week in Cork, Kieran Rose, contends that leafleting on Prince's Street in Cork's city centre served as a significant event for reasons of pragmatism, since 'Leafleting was the main activity because there were too few of us to organise a march.'[30] Rose also notes that the very 'publicness' of leafleting for gay rights on Prince's Street created a public presence, especially in a city that was at the time quite isolated. Hosting Pride events such as this brought diversity and new ideas into the city.[31] One of the significant demonstrations and activities as part of the Munster Gay Pride Week in 1981 was the installation of a giant pink triangle on top of the Comeragh Mountains by gay and lesbian activists from Cork and Waterford IGRMs, symbolising the unity of gay people in Munster in their fight for their civil liberties.[32]

Pride was very much a central feature of the early days of the fight for gay and lesbian civil rights. Following the conclusion of the Gay Pride festivities in 1982, and as summer turned to autumn, Declan Flynn, a young gay man, was 'queer-bashed' to death in Fairview Park in Dublin by a group of five young men. Following Flynn's murder, the five responsible received suspended sentences from Judge Seán Gannon, as he declared that Flynn's death 'could never be regarded as murder'. The outcome of this case ignited public outrage within

Ireland's gay and lesbian community, prompting the Stop Violence Against Gays and Women march, held on 19 March 1983. The sheer number of people who attended proved to be one of the most visible demonstrations of gay rights in Ireland. Following the righteous anger in the wake of Flynn's killing, Gay Pride Week 1983 was to be the first Pride event to involve a significant march through the main streets of Dublin, where 150 people walked from the Fusiliers' Arch at St Stephen's Green, through the newly pedestrianised Grafton Street, right up towards O'Connell Street. Since the case of Declan Flynn and Pride 1983, Pride marches have become the parades as we know them today and have become a mainstay of Pride season. However, the suite of social, cultural and political activities established by the Prides from 1974 to 1982 set in train the multiple components of what is now the Pride month of June.

Pride has continued to grow, change and evolve across the country. In 1990, activist Nuala Ward organised Galway's first Gay Pride parade; Belfast hosted its first Gay Pride Week in June 1991, with Limerick coming later in 2001 with theirs. Pride has migrated from large cities to smaller towns and counties, as communities come together to celebrate LGBTQ people. Pride remains an essential marker: it is an opportunity to challenge homophobic and transphobic legislation; it can change the hearts and minds of those who may hold an antagonistic position against sexual and gender minorities; and it is empowering and revelatory, particularly for younger and older closeted

LGBTQ people who are still not comfortable with themselves. Finally, Pride at its core is a transnational movement, aimed towards queer liberation for all – and is all the more potent as it is still a punishable offence to be gay in sixty-six countries around the world. Like the generation who revolted at Stonewall in New York in 1969, and those twelve Irish gays and lesbians who protested outside of the British embassy in 1974, Pride is not only an assertion of who we are, but also an assertion of hope and somewhere we can celebrate our wins and be angry at our losses, all while having a bit of fun and a party along the way.

7

The AIDS Priest
and His Ministry

The Story of Fr Bernárd Lynch

New York, 1982. On a sweltering summer's day Bernárd Lynch picked up the phone: it was his friend Stuart Garcia. It had been a while since the two men had seen each other, and Bernárd sensed a particular urgency in Stuart's voice, so he quickly made arrangements to meet him in Julius', a gay bar in Greenwich Village. He spotted Stuart across the room and went over to wrap him in a big hug, delighted to see his friend again. It was only when Bernárd stepped back that he saw the lesion on Stuart's neck. His stomach dropped: Kaposi's sarcoma. He knew what it meant. And so did Stuart, who asked Bernárd to be by his side for what he knew was to come.[1] Sitting in Julius' bar that day, the two friends understood that AIDS had become a crisis in the gay community in New York, and across the world, and that Stuart would soon be fighting for his life, like so many others around him.

Stuart and Bernárd met when they were studying at Columbia University. They first spotted each other on the athletics track where, one day, Stuart shouted out to Bernárd, in typical New York fashion, 'Hey, man, you've got very good legs!' Somewhat embarrassed, Bernárd thanked him for the compliment, before adding, 'And why did you admire my legs?' Stuart replied, 'Well, I'm gay.' 'Ah, that makes sense,' Bernárd began, before winking and adding, 'Well, I'm a priest, so I'm booked!'[2] While a romantic connection did not emerge, the two became extremely close friends over the course of their Columbia years and beyond.

As a number of AIDS-related illnesses began to take their toll, Stuart returned to his family in Austin, Texas, to be looked after. Bernárd went out to see him and found Stuart angry – in particular, angry at God – but determined that he was going to beat his illness. That was until one afternoon when, back working in New York at his AIDS ministry, Bernárd came home to find a desperate voice message on his answering machine from Stuart's mother, Nora, saying that Stuart had not long left, that he was fading fast and that he had asked for Bernárd to be by his side for his final moments. That night Bernárd flew to Austin for his second (and last) time, arriving at the hospital at midnight. On entering the room, he took his friend by the hand and simply said, 'Stuart, it's Bernárd – what can I do?' Squeezing his hand, Stuart whispered, 'Just be here.'[3] For the rest of that night, and until 6.30 the next evening, Bernárd sat on one side of the bed while Nora sat on the other, stroking Stuart's cheek, whispering, 'Stuart, my only son,' as her boy, and Bernárd's friend, passed from this world.

Stuart Garcia was only twenty-three when he died. He was academically brilliant and extremely good-looking, but taken all too soon. Bernárd performed the funeral, but did not even have time to mourn Stuart's passing, as he was already in the thick of a war that was ravaging the gay community in New York. Fr Lynch was, at the time, providing pastoral outreach and care for a community of gay people. His work with those living with and dying from AIDS brought him close to the edge of his physical and spiritual limits and also into direct conflict with the Catholic Church authorities he served, who sought to destroy him simply because he wanted to help young gay people prepare for their untimely deaths.

Fr Bernárd Lynch was born in 1947 in Ennis, County Clare, and educated at the local Christian Brothers School, where he developed an interest in becoming a Catholic priest at a very young age. Following his graduation from school in 1965, he joined the Society of African Missions before being admitted to a seminary in Northern Ireland, where he received his first taste of confronting power and oppression when he participated in civil disobedience to protest the unlawful killing of Catholics at the hands of the British government in Derry. Later, in June 1971, Bernárd was ordained a priest and sent on a mission to Zambia. During this period, Bernárd began to realise that he was gay. He was sent to Columbia University to do further studies in psychology and theology, where he learnt to come to terms with his position – that he was not simply a gay man, but a gay Catholic priest. The odds were stacked against him, given that the devotion to his vocation was innately in opposition to the Church's position on homosexuality, which maintained that being gay or lesbian was immoral. Bernárd needed to find community and like-minded people. He consulted the local *Yellow Pages* and to his surprise found Dignity, a group made up of gays and lesbians within the Roman Catholic Church whose goal was to change the Church's stance on homosexuality. The group had to meet in the Protestant Church of the Good Shepherd, since gay people were forbidden from congregating on Catholic property. When he started to attend the Dignity mass services, Bernárd was very much in the closet, as both a gay man and a priest, as he grappled with his internalised homophobia, guilt and shame. He hoped that attending Dignity services would help him on the road to being out and open.

Over the next number of months, Bernárd attended the Dignity church services incognito. That is, until one Saturday evening, when the priest who usually came to celebrate mass did not show up. As the realisation swept across the crowd of around two hundred gay and lesbian Catholics, Bernárd was overcome by his Catholic guilt. As he recalls, 'I'm sitting there saying in my head, *I'm a priest*. I don't know what came over me, but I turned to the guy next to me and I whispered, "I'm a priest." It was like a confession, and like a typical New Yorker, he shouts to the congregation, pointing at me, "He's a priest!"'[4] Outed to an entire congregation, Bernárd, nervous and shaking like a leaf, walked up to the altar and gave his first mass. He had found his gay Catholic family. He never looked back.

In 1978, he was made a campus minister at Mount Saint Michael Academy, a boys' school in the Bronx, where he taught and provided pastoral care to the students. This was to be his day job, which put food on the table and paid for his rent, while outside of his time at Mount Saint Michael he was doing all he could to progress the cause of Dignity. Bernárd became especially active and outspoken around the Church's attitude towards homosexuality. He marched openly and publicly, in clerical clothing, in the 1980 New York Pride parade alongside Dignity. All was going well until 1981, when Bernárd noticed that many of the gay men in Dignity were getting sick. One of the earliest people he recalls was a young man called Gustavo from Colombia, who became incredibly ill. Doctors had no idea what was wrong with him. Father Declan, a priest friend of Bernárd's, also became suddenly unwell, missing his words when giving his Palm Sunday mass, unable to see clearly. By the following Friday he was dead.[5] Soon Bernárd began to see gay men throughout his congregation and New York City suffer with the same symptoms. And then he began to see them die.

The New York Times reported on the unfurling phenomenon with the headline 'Rare Cancer Seen in 41 Homosexuals'.[6] In June 1981 the Centers for Disease Control and Prevention (CDC) similarly described the trend appearing around gay men getting sick, with the 'gay cancer' being dubbed Gay-Related Immune

Deficiency (GRIDS) before becoming formally known as AIDS in September 1982.[7] Seeing what was happening to the community, Bernárd became fearful. He wrote a will. He made the journey home to Clare to his parents, to explain to them as best he could what was going on with the little knowledge that he had. As he notes, 'New York and County Clare, they're a million miles apart.'[8]

Mass hysteria spread throughout the media in the early 1980s, suggesting that AIDS was airborne, that it could be passed through touching, sharing kitchen utensils and even sharing a toilet. As a result, many of the men with an AIDS diagnosis had nowhere to go and started reaching out to Bernárd for help. Headlines increased the moral panic swirling around the disease: 'AIDS Contact Fears from the Kiss of Life'; 'AIDS Warning to Organ Donors'; 'New Alert as AIDS Victims Increase'; 'Terror Hits Town after AIDS Death'; 'Victim of AIDS is Cremated in Secret'; and 'AIDS Fear Ban in Pub'.[9] AIDS then exploded as a news story when Hollywood actor and icon Rock Hudson, in July 1985, appeared, weak and visibly sick, in public for the first time in several weeks. As his health deteriorated, he flew to Paris for treatment, where his publicity team announced: 'Rock Hudson has AIDS'. It was later revealed that Hudson was gay, having lived much of his career in the closet due to the fear of his Hollywood career being destroyed if he came out.[10] Media coverage carried homophobic undertones and, finally, overt accusations, suggesting that it was not AIDS but homosexuality that was the killer disease.[11] AIDS became inexorably part of the larger discourse of retribution against gay men, with the media popularising the narrative of AIDS as an issue confined to specific groups – which included gay men, intravenous drug users and sex workers. This created the dichotomy of 'general population' versus 'risk groups', which served to further marginalise the groups but also brought them under intense media scrutiny.

Bernárd quickly realised that the men who reached out to him were being left to fend for themselves in the worst situations possible as they lay in their beds, sick and dying. 'I spent more time changing diapers, cleaning up the piss and shit of young men, than I did praying,' he later said.[12] As part of his pastoral care, Bernárd would also shop for the sick men, stay with them for the night if they felt lonely or even lie in the bed beside them so they could feel the touch of another person – many people were fearful of touching a person with AIDS. But Bernárd was living through a war and becoming overwhelmed. 'As a priest, I was spending more and more of my time visiting the sick, anointing the dying, officiating at funerals and finding my duties emotionally and physically draining,' he said.[13] In 1982, after pleading with his Dignity congregation for help, he established a Catholic AIDS ministry, the first of its kind in New York, which served those living and dying with AIDS and later HIV.

Bernárd began to see more and more men dying. One was in his twenties and had become estranged from his family as a result of his sexual identity. The estrangement continued, even when the family had been told the man had AIDS and was dying.[14] Following his death, a service was held in St Francis Xavier Church in Greenwich Village, a sympathetic church in the gay district of New York where an 'AIDS funeral' could be carried out, given that the Catholic Church would not allow such funerals in some places and would not allow the burial of bodies in the 'sacred' ground of their cemeteries. Many of the bodies of people who died with AIDS had to be cremated, and once Bernárd received the ashes of the young man who'd been estranged, he called the family one final time to see if they wanted their son's remains to spread themselves. But they wanted nothing to do with them, so to honour and commemorate his friend, Bernárd brought his ashes to Drumcliffe cemetery in Ennis and spread them over his mother's grave, who herself had recently passed away.[15]

In one instance, his AIDS ministry brought him into contact with Anthony Sofio, Elizabeth Taylor's former dressmaker and friend. Anthony had asked Bernárd to break the news to Elizabeth that he was dying. As Bernárd recalls: 'She was ever so courteous and kind, sending Anthony the most beautiful bouquet of orchids I have ever seen. She wrote on the card: *To dearest Anthony. I place my hand on your forehead and my head on your heart and wish you love. Elizabeth.*'[16]

The growing visibility of Bernárd's AIDS ministry drew significant attention, both in New York and Ireland, and he quickly became dubbed 'the AIDS priest' by the press.[17] When a young gay man died from AIDS, Bernárd was simply told by a member of a local Church authority to 'find a grave and bury him'.[18] Bernárd also began to see priests succumbing to various AIDS-related illnesses and witnessed first-hand their treatment at the hands of the Church. This left many of them with nowhere to go except for Bernárd's AIDS ministry. One such example was a close friend of Bernárd's, Fr Jeremy Mullins, who lived in New York. He became very sick and, having been cared for by Bernárd, flew to Florida to spend Christmas with his brother Bruce, who was also a priest. Over the course of this holiday, things shifted suddenly; Bruce intervened in the friendship and warned Bernárd that he was not to contact Jeremy again. Soon after this warning, Jeremy died and Bernárd was forbidden from attending his funeral by his family, with Bruce threatening to have the police remove him if he so much as showed his face. It was evident to Bernárd that blame was being put on him for Jeremy's death from AIDS.[19]

Bernárd encountered many Irish people over the course of his work. LGBTQ people often emigrated in search of a more supportive social climate and this was usually to metropolitan centres. The Irish cases were especially difficult for Bernárd as, more often than not, the men would not have come out to their families at home. On one occasion a young gay Irish man who was near the end of his life asked Bernárd to call his family. Bernárd rang the man's home landline, which his mother answered. He began to tell the woman that her son was sick, that things were not looking good and that she needed to get onto the next flight to New York. A few days later Bernárd waited nervously in the arrivals hall of John F. Kennedy International Airport and, seeing her emerge from the gate, gave her a wave. He brought her out to his car to drive her to the hospital, straight to her son. As she sat in the front seat, he took a deep breath and gently broke it to her that her son was gay. Her eyes filling with tears, she looked at Bernárd and asked, 'Please don't tell me my son has the Rock Hudson disease.'[20] Over the next number of days, Bernárd would help the mother and her son as they said goodbye to each other, before organising funeral arrangements. This was something that happened all too frequently – so many mothers making the dreaded journey across the Atlantic to say goodbye to their sons.

In 1984 Bernárd's ministry was recognised by the Mayor of New York, Ed Koch, who invited Bernárd to join the newly formed New York Taskforce on AIDS. In 1986 he testified before New York City Council regarding a bill designed to guarantee LGBT people the right to employment and housing without any discrimination relating to their sexual identity. Bernárd canvassed for this bill, as many vulnerable people with AIDS and HIV lost their jobs and were evicted onto the streets. Speaking out on the bill contributed to Bernárd's already significant public profile, as he opposed New York Cardinal John O'Connor's stance on the issue, with the media aiding and abetting a public spat between the two.[21]

Bernárd began to experience difficulties in his professional and personal life, especially at Mount Saint Michael Academy, with threats of reputational damage and litigation as a result of his AIDS activism. After an appearance on *The Phil Donahue Show*, 'a certain gentleman said that they would find a boy who would bring certain kinds of charges against me if I didn't stop'.[22] Threats such as these spiralled into what could be seen as a witch hunt when the brother of his priest friend, Jeremy, Fr Bruce Mullins, appeared outside his school with a sign that read: *Fr Lynch = Pervert. Do you want him near your sons?* Fr Mullins also distributed flyers to students and their teachers, denouncing Bernárd's AIDS ministry as evil and immoral. A small minority of teaching staff began a campaign in the school, mounting pressure on Bernárd to quit his job or risk being fired, which he refused to do. Three members of the teaching faculty formed SAFE (Students Against Faggots in Education), which eventually forced the hand of the school's principal to request Bernárd's resignation.

The tensions continued. As a result of the 'Halloween letter' of Cardinal Joseph Ratzinger (later Pope Benedict XVI), where he labelled gay people as 'disordered in their nature' and 'evil in their love',[23] Cardinal O'Connor subsequently moved to expel all members of Dignity from church property. Bernárd's AIDS ministry quickly came to an end, with the Archdiocese of New York effectively banning him from serving as a priest in the

US, and ordering him to Rome on sabbatical. During this year in Europe, the FBI continued their criminal investigation of an allegation of sexual abuse against Bernárd by a former student at Mount Saint Michael's. Bernárd's friends and colleagues told him that he was being made an example of by the archdiocese: 'If you go against us and if you are open in this way, this is what we will to do you.'[24] Bernárd was set on a collision course with two of the most formidable institutions in the world: the FBI and the Catholic Church.

To establish his innocence, Bernárd returned to New York to face the charges on 28 June 1988 – a move that the prosecution had not anticipated. On arriving in the US, he was arrested and detained and was held in the Bronx Supreme Court for twenty-four hours before being brought to the courtroom. As he recalls: 'When I went to the court after being held, I will never forget walking in, in between an FBI agent and an NYPD detective. I was in despair not knowing what was to come, but when they opened the door and I went in, the courthouse was packed, as those who I had helped, in Dignity, those living with AIDS, some of them in their final days, came to support me. In their worse moments, they were there. It was one of the most moving moments of my life.'[25] The charges against Bernárd were read by the judge. From that point, Bernárd met with his defence team as the prosecution and the defence deliberated on what form the trial would take. Eventually, a non-jury trial was agreed upon, opening in the South Bronx on 18 April 1989. But the case from the prosecution quickly fell apart. The charges of sexual abuse hinged solely on the testimony of one student, who had been coerced into making the false allegations, resulting in the case collapsing and the judge exonerating Bernárd of all charges.

Throughout the trial Bernárd continued to visit hospitals, to be at the bedsides of those living with AIDS and HIV and to help where he could. But by the end of the trial he was broken. In the ten years since starting his AIDS ministry and working with Dignity he had witnessed the loss of six hundred people, most of whom he had ministered to personally. The cost of helping each of these people, of being compassionate, caring and loving, was very high. Bernárd was seen as a pariah by the Church hierarchy and a problem to be dealt with: he lost his job, he was put on trial for crimes he never committed, he was spat upon and had drinks thrown on him in pubs. Yet despite these difficulties, Bernárd persisted in progressing the cause for those living with and dying from AIDS, along with trying make the Catholic Church an inclusive space for sexual diversity. And, despite the high personal cost of being 'the AIDS priest', he looks back on this title foisted upon him by the media and says, 'I wear that title as a badge of honour. I am the AIDS priest. I am proud of it. What I had seen and done with young gay men, I will wear it for the rest of my life with pride, with gratitude and humility. And as the AIDS priest, I will ensure that those we lost will never be forgotten. We must remember them.'[26] To date, more than 116,403 people have died from AIDS in New

York City alone, and Fr Bernárd Lynch led the charge to let these young gay men live and die with dignity.[27]

Since his time in New York, Bernárd had his relationship with Billy Desmond publicly blessed, in 1998, and in 2006 he became the first Catholic priest to enter a civil partnership. The couple legally married in Ireland in 2017, marking a historic moment in County Clare. Bernárd received accolades for his life's work, including a New York City Council Proclamation and the Presidential Distinguished Service Award for the Irish Abroad from President Michael D. Higgins. Notably, in 2023, he was honoured with a civic reception in County Clare, recognising his four-decade-long dedication to advocating for LGBTQIA+ individuals and his impactful support for those affected by HIV/AIDS during the pandemic. Bernárd continues his advocacy and ministry within these communities, culminating in the donation of his extensive activist archive to the National Library of Ireland in November 2022.

Close Encounters of a Hollywood Kind

*Rock Hudson and the
Early Irish Gay Scene*

The year 1968 was an eventful one. In the US, Dr Martin Luther King Jr's assassination in April was followed by that of Robert F. Kennedy in June, who was set to win the primaries to be the Democratic presidential candidate. In France, there were widespread student riots and civil unrest, bringing the economy of the nation to a standstill. Meanwhile in Ireland, the trappings of a State visit took up much of the May headlines when King Baudouin and Queen Fabiola of Belgium were honoured across the city in a series of State banquets, tree-planting ceremonies and attempts at playing hurling with President Éamon de Valera at the presidential residence, Áras an Uachtaráin. Elsewhere in the city, Michael Murtagh was sitting in Rice's pub, at the corner of St Stephen's Green and South King Street. Having clocked off early from his job in a nearby government department, Michael was enjoying the hour of peace and calm before the arrival of the evening crowd. That was until he looked towards the door, where a strangely familiar man was crossing the threshold. He was strikingly tall, with an extremely broad chest and a handsome, chiselled face. Nonchalantly walking towards the bar, the man asked for a pint of Guinness in a deep, velvety midwestern US accent. He smiled at Michael, who suddenly realised who this dazzling man before him was: Rock Hudson, one of Hollywood's biggest stars.[1]

Born Roy Harold Scherer Jr in 1925, and having served in the navy during World War II, he later pursued a career in Hollywood as an actor, where he was given the name Rock Hudson – deriving from a combination of the Rock of Gibraltar and the Hudson River to convey a strong sense of masculinity through his star image.[2] Tall, dark and handsome, Hudson epitomised the Hollywood ideal of American masculinity of the 1950s and 1960s. He starred in a series of movie hits, including *All That Heaven Allows* (1955) and *Giant* (1956), receiving an Academy Award nomination for best actor for the latter. Starring in a series of romantic comedies alongside Doris Day, Hudson became 'the man that women wanted to marry and the man the men said they'd like to be'.[3] However, behind the sheen of Hollywood celebrity, Rock Hudson lived his life as a gay man, hidden under a constructed heterosexuality engineered by Hollywood agents, producers and directors. Hudson's public 'closetedness' was to ensure that his career was protected from any homophobic ramifications, which may have risked him losing work as an actor and being publicly shamed for his sexual identity.

In 1968, Hudson was working on the musical film *Darling Lili*, alongside Julie Andrews, with some of the scenes being filmed in the Gaiety Theatre in the heart of Dublin. In between production shoots, Hudson sought to sample Dublin's then underground gay scene – which was how he came to join Michael, with his pint, in the front bar of Rice's pub, which had earned itself a reputation as a 'gay pub' from six o'clock onwards every evening.[4] Rice's was located at the corner of 141 St Stephen's Green and 2 South King Street. As Sam McGrath writes, Rice's had two bars on ground level with separate entrances, with the front bar section becoming a friendly space for Dublin's lesbian and gay community. In the late 1960s Rice's was sometimes called the 'geriatric ward' by younger gay men.[5]

In awe of the Hollywood royalty before him, Michael was unsure that Hudson knew where he was. While venues during the 1960s would not have been advertised overtly as gay-friendly, Michael anticipated that Hudson would soon realise what kind of place he was in when Rice's usual evening clientele began to fill up the venue. However, Hudson pulled up a chair beside Michael and started to chat about how beautiful Ireland was, talking about the film he was making with Julie Andrews and just striking up general conversation. Michael, stunned, tried to play things casually and treat the interaction just like any kind of random encounter in a bar. As time progressed and as more drinks were consumed, the bar began to fill up with gay men, with Hudson checking out each one. Quickly, Michael realised that his new-found

Hollywood friend knew exactly where he was and what he was doing. Hudson invited Michael to accompany him to a party in the Gaiety Theatre that Friday, but unfortunately he was not in a position to do so. As Michael left the bar that night, he was in shock: here was the screen love interest of Doris Day, in Ireland, looking for romance with an Irish man.[6]

While Hudson's sexuality was an open secret in production circles in LA, the broader public – and particularly the Irish – were completely unaware that he was gay. Over the course of that week of the film's production, Hudson also visited Bartley Dunne's on 32 Stephen Street Lower, another prominent gay-friendly establishment, much to the awe and surprise of the patrons within. Bartley Dunne's, along with Rice's, was one of the more popular bars where gay people would congregate in the 1960s and 1970s, to the extent that international visitors such as Rock Hudson could seek out these spaces and find community. Bartley Dunne's had begun to attract a gay clientele in the 1950s. David Norris recalls visiting the bar when he emerged on the scene in the early 1970s: 'It was an Aladdin's cave to me, its wicker-clad Chianti bottles stiff with dribbled candle wax, tea chests covered in red-and-white chequered cloths, heavy scarlet velvet drapes and an immense collection of multicoloured liqueurs glinting away in their bottles. The place was [full] of theatrical old queens, with the barmen clad in bum-freezer uniforms.'[7]

Jim Dunne recalled meeting Hudson in Bartley Dunne's: 'My wife and I were introduced to Hudson

... He was an unbelievably handsome man. The kind that would have women running after him.' However, as Jim notes, it was not women who were approaching him in Bartley Dunne's, but guys: 'He lapped it up ... he was Rock Hudson and everybody knew he was Rock Hudson. He liked that.'[8] Jim realised that Hudson, the romantic icon of this time, was in a gay bar making no pretence that he was straight. Because the US press relentlessly pursued Hudson in an attempt to out him, there are very few photos of Hudson with other men, particularly any boyfriends that he had over the years. Most pictures were publicity shots or featured women who were his supposed 'lovers'. On the Irish gay scene, while many were clearly enamoured with him, he was left relatively alone by the press. The week-long trip to Ireland included a visit to the Blarney Stone in Cork, but was predominantly concentrated in Dublin. On one of his final nights, which he had spent with Jim Dunne, a number of men in Bartley Dunne's began to fight over who would get to go home with Hudson. As Dunne recalls, 'In the end he sat in the back of his limo, which was parked directly outside the pub, with the door ajar, waiting for whomever won the fight to go with him back to the Gresham.'[9] While a night of romance, passion and fun ensued, Hudson got a flight back to LA the next day, leaving many star-struck Irish men in awe – not just of his handsome good looks, but because it signified to them there were other gay people out there in positions of power and celebrity, albeit usually closeted.

The story of Rock Hudson and his sojourn in Dublin's early and burgeoning gay scene demonstrates the centrality and importance of queer spaces. His very presence and the lack of a significant media event or scandal (aside from the various suitors across Bartley Dunne's and Rice's) shows the underground and hidden nature of Ireland's early gay scene. The criminal laws in place, and a general climate of homophobia, along with the morally conservative ethos of the Catholic Church in Ireland, compelled gay and lesbian spaces to function in the shadows, meaning that these early bars were perfect sites for high-profile figures or celebrities like Rock Hudson, who sought privacy within these spaces. McGrath describes the gay social scene in Dublin from 1923 to 1973 as encompassing 'subterranean gay-friendly bars and spaces'.[10] While the Gresham Hotel on O'Connell Street and the Shelbourne on Stephen's Green were known as meeting places for middle-class gay men, other spaces, such as the United Arts Club, which had rooms, a bar and dining facilities at 3 Fitzwilliam Street Upper, were spaces where gay men tended to congregate.[11] Paul Candon commented that the emergence of any kind of gay scene at the start of the twentieth century was 'largely concentrated around the theatre circles, the opera. Suede shoes were the badge of recognition.' Candon also describes how the opening of 'Parisian-style pissoirs' in Dublin in preparation for the Eucharistic Congress of 1932 resulted in public toilets becoming a frequent space for gay men to have sex.[12]

Throughout the 1930s and 1940s, a growing number of pubs in the city started to establish themselves as attracting partly a gay clientele. McGrath contends that Davy Byrnes on Duke Street, founded in 1889, was one of the first documented pubs to have an established gay patronage; in the 1930s it became a hotspot for gay people involved in production and acting in the Theatre Royal nearby. McGrath speculates that the original proprietor, Davy Byrne himself, may have been gay, given that he was buried in Glasnevin cemetery with his friend Thomas Campbell.[13] In the 1950s, the backroom of Davy Byrnes became particularly popular amongst men, but cruising through eye contact was the only sort of flirtation that could occur, as physical contact had to be hidden from the barmen.[14] Davy Byrnes would continue to be a frequent haunt for gay men until the emergence of a more visible gay scene. In the late 1940s The Catacombs, a basement flat in 13 Fitzwilliam Place, became a popular place for when the pub closed and was renowned for its sexual licence, with Brendan Behan noting it as a space where 'men had women, men had men and women had women'.[15]

Rice's and Bartley Dunne's were both crucial stepping stones for many in the gay community. As Maurice Clarke says, 'Bartley Dunne's and Rice's [were] bars that you just have a few drinks in to work up the courage to go for a dance.'[16] Terri Blanche recalls that these early gay bars were vital incremental milestones for young gay and lesbian people coming out in the 1970s and 1980s: 'I remember seeing guys and women coming into

'Let Gays In' protest, 28 September 1981. Tonie Walsh picketing the US embassy in Dublin as part of a global protest against anti-gay immigration legislation. (Thomas A. O'Shea, Irish Queer Archive. Courtesy of the National Library of Ireland.)

PARENTS OF GAYS LOVE THEIR CHILDREN

● Something to think about . . . A banner in the crowd attending the rally held by the Dublin Gay Collective

Phil Moore, holding a sign saying 'Parents of Gays Love their Children' at the Stop Violence Against Gays and Women Fairview march. (Irish Queer Archive. Courtesy of the National Library of Ireland.)

Phil Moore joins protestors outside Leinster House at an action over the lack of gay law reform progress in October 1992. (Christopher Robson Photographic Collection. Courtesy of the National Library of Ireland.)

GAY COMMUNITY NEWS

IRELAND'S LESBIAN AND GAY NEWSPAPER · AUGUST 1993 · MONTHLY · FREE

ON WEDNESDAY JULY 7, 1993, THE PRESIDENT OF IRELAND, MRS MARY ROBINSON, SIGNED INTO LAW, THE BILL WHICH DECRIMINALISES HOMOSEXUAL ACTS BETWEEN ADULTS OF 17 YEARS AND OVER.

Kieran Rose, Chris Robson of GLEN, Phil Moore of Parents Enquiry and Suzy Byrne of GLEN celebrate outside Dáil Eireann after the legislation was passed.

Inside issue 54

y Pride 3
fficial endorses celebra-
f lesbian and gay pride

sidestep 4
tisfaction all round as
s reneges

Sex 5
ever know what you could

The GCN interview 6
The Editor and GLEN have
it out

London murders 8
Suspect charged with two
murders

Photospread 10/11
Pride caught on camera

GCN Classifieds 16/17
The people, places and
things on offer

Postbox 18
Complaints and comments

Listings 19
What, where and when

Gay Community News front page featuring Kieran Rose, Christopher Robson, Phil Moore and Suzy Byrne celebrating the change of legislation on 24 June 1993. (Irish Queer Archive. Courtesy of the National Library of Ireland.)

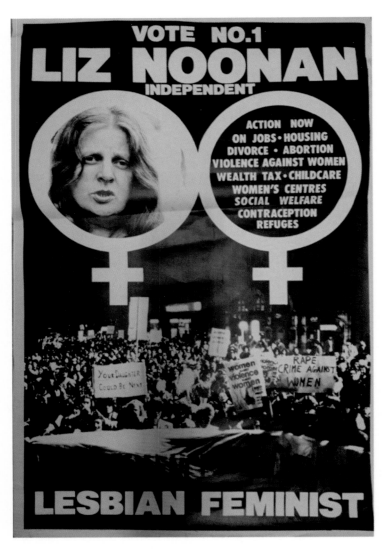

Liz Noonan campaign poster for contesting the 1981 general election.
(Cathal Kerrigan personal archive. Courtesy of Cathal Kerrigan.)

EQUAL RIGHTS FOR EVERYONE!
- GAY & LESBIAN EQUALITY CAMPAIGN -

By law, the next Dail must introduce new legislation following the Norris Decision in the European Court of Human Rights.

WE CALL FOR:
- Anti-discrimination laws in housing and in jobs for all minorities in Ireland.
- No discrimination in the courts against lesbian mothers or gay fathers.
- A single age of consent for everyone.
- Single people to be able to transfer their pension rights to a person of their choice.
- Comprehensive sex education in all schools.
- Support for health, advice, and information services that provide full, non-directive, counselling.

VOTE 15th JUNE
TONIE WALSH
DUBLIN SOUTH EAST

PLEASE GIVE US YOUR *1ST PREFERENCE*, AND THEN YOUR NEXT PREFERENCES TO CANDIDATES LIKELY TO IMPLEMENT OUR PROGRAMME.

GAY SWITCHBOARD DUBLIN - 544855
LESBIAN LINE - 613777 (Thurs. 7-9 pm)
Campaign HQ: Gay Switchboard, 13 Christchurch Place, Dublin 8.

Tonie Walsh's 1989 general election campaign flyer. (Irish Queer Archive. Courtesy of the National Library of Ireland.)

Eamon Somers (left) and Owen Conroy (right) distributing leaflets and pink carnations during Gay Pride Week 1980. (Don Wood Collection, shared with permission from the collection's custodian Karl Hayden.)

 **GAY PRIDE WEEK
20:28 JUNE 81**

GAY RIGHTS ARE HUMAN RIGHTS

5 to 10% OF THE IRISH POPULATION IS GAY

• OVER 6,000 IN CORK ALONE

IRELAND IS THE ONLY EUROPEAN COUNTRY WHICH STILL LEGISLATES • AGAINST GAYS

WE DEMAND SOCIAL AND LEGAL EQUALITY NOW!

GAY RIGHTS NOW!

Information leaflet distributed during Cork Gay Pride Week 1981. (NLGF Collection, Irish Queer Archive. Courtesy of the National Library of Ireland.)

Information leaflet distribution during Cork Gay Pride Week 1981.
(Kieran Rose personal archive. Courtesy of Kieran Rose.)

GLEN banner held by Fergus McGarvey and Suzy Byrne at Dublin
Pride 1993. (Christopher Robson Photographic Collection. Courtesy
of the National Library of Ireland.)

Celebration of the decriminalisation of homosexuality in Ireland, on the steps of the Central Bank Plaza, Dame Street, during Dublin Pride March 1993. (Christopher Robson Photographic Collection. Courtesy of the National Library of Ireland.)

(L–R): Fr John McNeill, Fr Bernárd Lynch, Fr Dan McCarthy and Rev Robert Carter marching in New York Pride 1980 in front of the Dignity banner. (Bernárd Lynch personal archive. Courtesy of Bernárd Lynch.)

Cathal Kerrigan and Máirtín Mac an Ghoill, founders of Gays Against Imperialism. (Cathal Kerrigan personal archive. Courtesy of Cathal Kerrigan.)

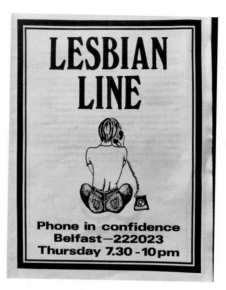

Belfast Lesbian Line poster. (Claire Hackett personal archive. Courtesy of Claire Hackett.)

Two flyers for the Gay Liberation Society from the early to mid-1970s at Queen's University Belfast. (Hugo McManus Collection, Irish Queer Archive. Courtesy of the National Library of Ireland.)

MUNSTER GCN

MUNSTER'S LESBIAN & GAY NEWSPAPER   FREE   MAY 1992

Lesbian mother wins custody battle

In an historic decision recently a lesbian mother living in rural Ireland in an openly lesbian relationship was granted custody of her two children, aged ten and six.

The decision was the end of a long dispute about custody between the woman and the husband she left some years ago. The judge relied on a long and detailed report from a social worker in reaching his verdict. The report far from fudging the facts gave "graphic detail" according to the solicitor in the case.

The mother expressed her delight and relief when the judge having spent fifteen minutes in court reading the report announced his verdict: "joint custody, the children to reside with their mother".

A full report of the case will appear in the May edition of the Cork based "Irish Women's News".

Lesbian mothers are everywhere

LOAFERS BAR

26 DOUGLAS ST., CORK

WATERSTONE'S BOOKSELLERS

49 Patrick Street, Cork.
Tel: (021) 276522.
Fax: (021) 276253.

Stockist of
Lesbian and Gay Titles
(in Gender Studies Dept.)

Limerick's Gay Bar...red

The White House, long established as Limerick's main lesbian and gay friendly pub, has barred most of its gay customers in recent weeks.

Problems with the White House have existed for some time. It closed temporarily in March and when it re-opened the new management made their anti-lesbian and gay policy very clear. Just before we went to print most of the membership of BLUSH walkedout to make whoever of their number was refused service!

There have been no protests to date at the new policy and some gay people still frequent the bar but there is mounting anger at the barring.

BLUSH

Meanwhile Braces Liberties Undoing Sexism and Homophobia (BLUSH) will be launched on the streets of Limerick on Saturday the 25th of April. The group plans a day of action in support of 'Condom Sense' campaign.

BLUSH is the new group formed from the old 'Lesbian and Gay Society' of Limerick University. The decision to re-name the society was covered in our April issue.

BLUSH has seen an influx of new, active members following its launch. BLUSH feels that its new format works better for students and young people generally. "Young people are often unsure about their sexual identity

and will get involved in a group like BLUSH when they won't join a Lesbian and Gay Society. We think the group will be much more effective than the old society."

Lines

There is good news about the future of the Limerick lesbian and gay lines. Rumours of crises are exaggerated. Fund-raising for the lines are in hand and a recruitment drive is planned for the near future.

New Meeting

Meanwhile regular "information-style" meetings are planned for Limerick. The new initiative came from discussions at the Gay and Lesbian Equality Network (GLEN) meeting in Dublin on the 9th of April.

The first event will take place in Limerick on the 15th of June. For information on venue and other details phone your local lesbian or gay information line.

Munster GCN front page news story covering the outcome of Toni Burgess's custody case. (*Gay Community News* Archive. Courtesy of *Gay Community News*.)

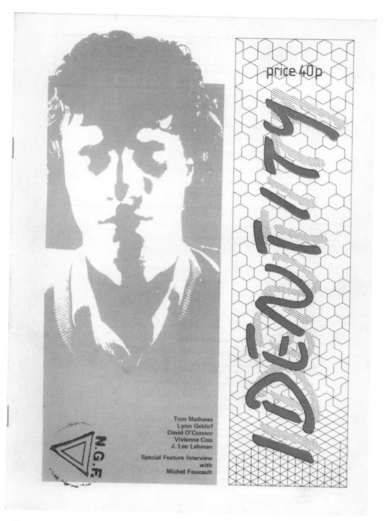

Identity magazine, which some booksellers and newsagents refused to distribute because lesbian and gay people appeared on the cover. (Irish Queer Archive. Courtesy of the National Library of Ireland.)

free free free

COMMUNITY NEWS

november '90 issue 24

24

OUTWAVES
Threat to silence programme

BY A *GCN* REPORTER

GCN has uncovered an attempt to force off the air Ireland's first lesbian and gay radio series, *OUTWAVES*. A little-known organisation called The Council of Social Concern has written to advertisers on Horizon Radio warning of the consequences of supporting the station. The letter urges advertisers to force the Bray-based community radio station to stop transmitting the programme.

The letter also accuses Horizon of: "actively supporting the very politicised homosexual lobby" and of submitting: "listeners of all ages, especially teenagers, to homosexual propaganda which is one-sided and unbalanced". It describes the programme as: "most unhealthy and abnormal". It claims that: "advertisers have a right, and duty, to determine [the station's] ethos and influence", and goes on to threaten: "you might like to consider whether it is in your company's best interests to be associated with a programme which is so offensive and potentially damaging."

SOCIALLY CONCERNED?

The letter is addressed to "Chief Executives/Managing Directors of advertisers on Horizon Radio" and comes from the Council of Social Concern, using an address at Sandbrook House, Stradbrook Lawn, Blackrock, Co. Dublin. One letter was received by an advertiser on Monday October 8, but Sandbrook House did not exist then; it had already been demolished. The same house was also used as its headquarters by The Society for the Protection of the Unborn Child (SPUC). It is believed to be owned by the PV Doyle Group.

The Council describes itself as being: "composed of authorised delegates from socially concerned groups and associations, for the purpose of communicating, co-ordinating and supporting the activities of its constituent organisations". Efforts to find out what "socially concerned groups and associations" are involved have proved fruitless, but an investigation by the *Sunday Tribune* (March 3 1985) revealed that the Council of Social Concern was formed in 1976. Its co-founder was a John O'Reilly, a former Knight of Columbanus and a leading light in both Family Solidarity and PLAC (the Pro-Life Amendment Campaign), which campaigned to have the so-called "pro-life" amendment inserted into the Constitution by Referendum in 1983. He was also secretary of Responsible Society, being credited as the brains behind the the whole pro-amendment campaign.

Another link between the Council of Social Concern and the Knights of Columbanus is Niall Darragh, understood to be a leading Knight, and chairman of the

Colin Wall, one of the presenters of

Council. The Community Standards Association also shared that address with the Council of Social Concern in Blackrock, they appear also to share a typewriter?

Other sources suggested to *GCN* that the Knights of Columbanus were planning a letter-writing campaign to Independent Radio and Television Commission Chairman Mr Justice Henchy, urging that *Outwaves* be discontinued. By coincidence, Mr Justice Henchy was one of the minority on the Supreme Court which disagreed with the ruling against David Norris in 1983. That ruling forced Senator Norris to take his case to the European Court of Human Rights. It took a further five years to achieve justice.

SECRETIVE BODY

The Knights of Columbanus is a secretive conservative Catholic lay-body, often likened to the Freemasons, and with headquarters in Ely Place, Dublin (*near Shaft nightclub*).

The letter to Horizon's advertisers is signed by a Sean Ryan who describes himself in the letter as "Chairman – Media-affairs", though other documents which have come into the possession of *GCN* describe him as "Media Secretary". The signature of Sean Ryan varies considerably from one document to another (see facsimiles page 3) and indeed one document has the signature Sean Ryan above the typed name Sean Byrne, indicating perhaps an identity crisis! *Gay Community News* has been unable to contact the Sean Ryan/Sean Byrne whose name appears.

MOST SINISTER

The letter to advertisers quotes an IMS Poll supposedly indica-

it likely that a similar proportion of your potential customers would likewise find such programmes [as *Outwaves*] distasteful and avoid those who support them?". Mr Ryan finds the 'most sinister' aspect of the programme to be the 'friendly-word' slot, provided by Philip, a counsellor with Gay Switchboard Dublin, where he claims: "confused youths are assured that they may be 'gay' and are given the names and addresses of what are euphemistically called 'befriending agencies'".

GCN can now reveal that the Council of Social Concern wrote to Board members of Horizon Radio in September to inform them that the effect of *Outwaves* is: "to glamourise an unnatural lifestyle which is anything but glamorous, and that the series was: "glorifying and romanticising the homosexual lifestyle". The Council claimed that the station had a duty to provide a series on the same day, and of the same duration, which would: "deal with the public health dangers of homosexual practices, psychiatric views on 'causes and cures' and how to treat young people with troubles in this area" The letter further insinuated that the fact that homosexual practices were illegal somehow made the programme illegal, even erroneously claiming that the Strasbourg ruling could have no effect here as our Supreme Court found our homophobic laws constitutional (the Law Reform Commission Report explicitly stated that the Supreme Court ruling here would not prevent the Dáil from making the necessary legal changes). The idea that the programme could be illegal was quashed when earlier complaints to the Independent Radio and Tele-

REVENUE

It is not yet known how many advertisers have received letters and Horizon's director Adrian Kennedy has declined to comment on the effect, if any, which the letters have had on advertising revenue. While it is known that Horizon is committed to serving the broadest range of interests in its community and would hope to resist this American-style intimidation of a letter-writing campaign, it could be assumed that any threat to the finances of a new radio station would pose serious problems, an assumption that CSC has no doubt made.

The danger of unrepresentative pressure groups and/or advertisers placing undue pressure on and influencing the policy of independent and local radio stations may not have been foreseen when the structures for local radio were being set up. The campaign against *Outwaves* raises the broader question: how independent *is* independent radio? It is a problem which the Independent Radio and Television Commission may need to address.

GCN front page news story covering the censorship threat against the Outwaves LGBT radio programme. (*Gay Community News* Archive. Courtesy of *Gay Community News*.)

Mr Pussy and Linda Martin announce the results of Alternative Miss Ireland I held at Sides dance club, Dublin, on April Fool's Day 1987. Seated (L–R): unnamed, 3rd prize; Miss Isle (Joe Campbell), winner; Miss Demeanour Rathmines (Tonie Walsh), 2nd prize. (Seán Gilmartin, Irish Queer Archive. Courtesy of the National Library of Ireland.)

Alternative Miss Ireland I, April Fool's Day 1987. Mr Pussy and Linda Martin keep the crowd entertained between contestants. (Seán Gilmartin, Irish Queer Archive. Courtesy of the National Library of Ireland.)

Bartley Dunne's with their girlfriend or their boyfriend and a year later ... they would show up as a gay person coming out.'[17] People would use these bars to test the scene and ensure that there was a community out there for them. As Bill Foley notes, both Bartley Dunne's and Rice's would serve as part of an early version of a 'gay pub crawl' of sorts and a regular part of socialisation on the early Irish gay and lesbian scene.[18] Even though these bars served as spaces for gays and lesbians to congregate, an amount of subterfuge was still required for demonstrating romantic or sexual interest in each other. 'It was all very nudge, nudge, wink, wink and a nod. The pint and the little wink as they're having the pint. It was all very coded,' Maurice Clarke recalls.[19]

Gay and lesbian spaces eventually popped up across the city under the guise of coded queerness, as club nights, members' clubs and often just gay-friendly. Many of these venues were run by straight men. As Jeremy Atherton Lin says, 'A gay bar can be a repository for all the extra that doesn't fit into other spaces,'[20] and as Elizabeth Lapovsky Kennedy and Madeline Davis explain, gay bars 'provide a place for socialization, [a] means of maintaining social cohesion, a context for each individual to confirm gay identity'.[21] The ways in which gay and lesbian spaces emerged in Dublin, and Ireland more broadly, was reflective of what Mickey Lauria and Lawrence Knopp describe as 'a spatial response to a historically specific form of oppression'.[22] The sporadic nature and lack of sustainable open and visible queer spaces can be attributed to the oppressive criminal laws, which made gay sex punishable. Between 1962 and 1972 there were 455 convictions of men in Ireland for crimes such as 'indecency with males' and 'gross indecency', and between 1940 and 1978 an average of thirteen men a year were jailed for homosexual offences.[23] This oppressive climate did not engender overt expression of diverse sexual identities in public in Ireland yet, as gay former San Francisco Supervisor Harry Britt asserted, sexuality and space are inextricably linked: 'When gays are spatially isolated, they are not gay because they are invisible.'[24]

Gay bars in Ireland had an important function during the mid twentieth century in socialisation and developing a lesbian and gay culture – and they still do today. They provided sanctuaries for international visitors, such as the publicly closeted Rock Hudson, to enjoy the freedom of sexual expression without fear of abuse or persecution, while also providing a crucial place for gay and lesbian people to meet and connect. While these bars were essential half a century ago, they remain necessary today – despite the fact that these spaces are in decline globally and in Ireland especially (Ireland's oldest gay bar, Loafers, closed in 2015). Gay bars, no matter where in the world, provide a sense of community, romance and connection, however ephemeral, to everyone, from a young person coming out of the closet to the Hollywood star taking a break between shoots.

9

Defiance and Defence

The Gay Defence Committee,
Police Harassment and the Murders of 1982

At 6.30 in the morning of 1 March 1982, Cathal Kerrigan is sound asleep in bed beside his boyfriend, Máirtín Mac an Ghoill. The creeping sunlight begins to emerge through the net curtain of their downstairs bedroom at Windsor Avenue in Fairview, Dublin. The quiet of the morning is abruptly shattered by ferocious knocking at the door. Cathal and Máirtín wake up and look at each other, bewildered. There's more violent pounding on the door. Máirtín scrambles out of the bed and starts putting on whatever clothes he can find. 'It's the gardaí,' he whispers to Cathal, who follows suit, throwing on clothes. Cathal gets to the front door and places his right foot behind it in case he needs to block entry. Slowly he opens the door, holding it slightly ajar. In front of him are four gardaí, two of whom are brandishing Uzi sub-machine guns, with two squad cars behind them. Trying to keep an air of calm in the face of what they felt was already an extremely heightened situation, Cathal asked, 'Can I help you?' One of the armed gardaí barked, 'We're here for Cathal Kerrigan and Máirtín Mac an Ghoill.' 'Have you got a search warrant?' Cathal responded. Through the crack in the door, the garda showed a warrant, so reluctantly Cathal opened the door and they stormed in and began searching the house. The other housemates, having heard the commotion, had ventured onto the landing only to have armed gardaí push past them, upending furniture and pulling out drawers. Storming back down to the kitchen, one garda announced that they were arresting Cathal and Máirtín, then dragged them out of the house. As they were pulled over the threshold towards the squad car, Cathal shouted back to his housemates, 'Call a solicitor. Now!'[1]

After being taken to a garda station on the other side of the city, Cathal was placed in a holding cell away from Máirtín and interrogated. It quickly became clear that this was a homophobically charged arrest. While it had been stated to the two men that they were being arrested under the Offences Against the State Act, for a crime vaguely referred to as some kind of robbery – which they were in no way connected to and for which they both had alibis – the interview quickly descended into intimidation and inappropriate questions about their lives together. The interrogation took place over the course of two ninety-minute sessions. Cathal's solicitor was not present for the first interrogation, as he was trying to find out which station Cathal was in. In that first session, while Cathal refused to answer any questions unrelated to the charges he was accused of, he recalls that taunts began to emerge from the gardaí. 'The state of you pair of bumboys,' one of them said. 'What do you even get up to in the bedroom?' came another. 'Which one of you is the man and which one is the woman?' 'What will your family make of this when they find out what you do be getting up to?'[2] At one point, a garda grabbed Cathal by his belt buckle, and he started to hyperventilate out of sheer panic. Gardaí continued to question him on his private life while humiliating him about his sexuality. At another point, the questioning garda asked him to provide his fingerprints and photographs. Cathal responded that he was not legally obliged to do so. Despite his protests, Cathal recalls that gardaí forced him to provide them. After being detained in a cell and questioned, his solicitor eventually arrived and was present for the second interrogation, immediately noting the unlawful nature of the arrest.

As Cathal left the station that evening, he reflected that he had known it would only be a matter of time before the gardaí came knocking. After the brutal murder of Charles Self on 21 January 1982 the gardaí had launched an extensive investigation into the gay community in Dublin, initiating a campaign of relentless surveillance and targeted harassment, doorstepping gay men and questioning them. Such was the level of intimidation that Cathal felt that something had to be done to protect the gay community, and so, with a number of other activists, he would soon set about establishing the Gay Defence Committee (GDC).

Charles Self, a 33-year-old Scottish man, was a talented set designer at RTÉ. He was responsible for crafting the sets of various shows, including the flagship *The Late Late Show*. Charles lived in Monkstown with his RTÉ colleague Vincent Hanley and frequented many of Dublin's gay spaces. January 1982 had been particularly cold, with heavy snow. On the evening of 20 January, with the snow having thawed throughout the day, Charles left work at RTÉ to pop into the Bailey and then Bartley Dunne's, before getting a taxi from Burgh Quay with a man later described by the taxi driver as having grey hair. The pair went back to Charles's house in Monkstown. A colleague of Charles's, Berty Tyrer, who was also a designer in RTÉ, was staying in Vincent Hanley's room at the time, as Vincent was away with work. Tyrer had been woken in the middle of the night by a man who came into his bedroom at around 2.30 a.m. and then quickly left after saying, 'Sorry, wrong room.'[3] Tyrer went back to sleep and then got up the next morning to find Charles dead, his body lying at the foot of the stairs. Tyrer had heard no commotion over the course of the night. He called the gardaí, who quickly arrived at the crime scene, described as 'absolute chaos' and the murder being noted as vicious. Charles had been stabbed fourteen times with an eight-inch kitchen knife.[4] State pathologist John Harbison concluded that Self had died from wounds to his neck and back. In his statement to the gardaí, Tyrer provided a sketch of the man who had come into his room, aiming to help the gardaí with their investigation. On the morning of 25

January, following the post-mortem on Charles's body, a service took place in St Andrew's Presbyterian Church in Blackrock in front of a congregation full of his friends and RTÉ colleagues, before he was flown that night back to his native Glasgow, where his funeral would take place. A garda investigation was quickly mounted in the days following Charles's murder from Pearse Street Garda Station, with thirty detectives assigned to investigate the case.

As initial leads fell away without producing any breakthroughs in the case, attention turned towards the gay community and, unfortunately, 'It became clear that the investigation was more concerned with compiling a file on gay men than it was with solving the murder.'[5] The Charles Self investigation resulted in the interrogation, photographing and fingerprinting of nearly 1,500 gay men at Pearse Street Garda Station.[6] Many of these interviews had little relevance to Charles Self or to his murder but delved deeply into the private lives of those being questioned. Gay men were asked about their sexual partners, their circle of gay friends, and were pressured to disclose their names and addresses to the gardaí.[7] Gardaí would frequently show up at gay pubs or wait outside as they closed, approaching gay men and compelling them to accompany them to the garda station for what were often invasive and intrusive questions. Refusal to comply sometimes led to threats, with gardaí warning individuals that they might visit their workplaces or homes. In some instances, these threats were carried out. This sustained harassment created a climate of fear, prompted by the constant dread of being forcibly outed. Ultimately, the initial fear of a murderer at large was overshadowed by the fear of garda intimidation.

The GDC would emerge in the wake of this investigation and was the product of alternative left-wing politics in the broader Irish gay civil rights movement. During a Gays Against Imperialism (GAI) meeting, which focused on highlighting the nationalist struggle in Northern Ireland and emphasised that gay liberation was intertwined with national liberation, Cathal, Máirtín and several other like-minded individuals came to a consensus.[8] They decided to form a group with a specific mission: empowering gay men to stand up against the ongoing harassment.[9] Prominent participants in the GDC included Bill Foley, Christopher Robson, Melissa Murray, Maura Molloy, Clodagh Boyd and Mick Quinlan. Following a GAI meeting, the first GDC meeting was held at Trinity College Dublin. From the outset, the leaders of the GDC were committed to establishing coalitions and alliances as a cornerstone of their activism. They reached out to members of organisations such as the Irish Council for Civil Liberties (ICCL), GAI, Prisoners' Rights Organisation (PRO) and People's Democracy to seek guidance on developing protective measures for the LGBTQ+ community.

Yet even as the GDC was being established, another homophobically charged killing took place. On 7 March 1982, George Leonard, a seventy-year-old music teacher living in Drimnagh, Dublin, was murdered.[10] The man responsible for this, John Carew, turned himself in to the gardaí, stating that he killed George because he had made an unwanted sexual advance,[11] using what became known as the 'gay panic defence' to explain why he had committed the murder. The gay panic defence refers to a situation in which a heterosexual individual charged with a violent crime against a gay person claims that they lost control and reacted violently because of an unwanted sexual advance.

The GDC had three key aims. Firstly, it intended to give direct leadership to the gay community and provide a cohesive response to the police harassment. Secondly, it sought to harness the power of visibility and publicity, through street action and protest, to bring the general public's attention what was perceived as garda aggression. Thirdly, it wanted to build a radical left-wing alternative of gay and lesbian liberatory politics. The organisation, as one of its co-founders notes, did not 'believe gay rights could just be achieved simply by changing the law – true liberation could only happen by building allied links with other organisations'.[12] As a result, strategic coalitions were considered central to its plans. The marginalisation and oppression of certain groups encouraged the development of alliance-building across the political left. Mutual marginality served as a significant means for the GDC to make a number of links with these groups, many of them active within republican politics. The coalitional approach in the case of the GDC reveals how systems of power and oppression interact to produce shared solidarity around building for social change. The GDC accordingly linked in with the ICCL, PRO, the H-Block Armagh campaign and feminist groups.

This approach was particularly effective in one of the GDC's first overt public demonstrations: a public picket of Pearse Street Garda Station, the headquarters of the Charles Self investigation. The picket was announced and advertised the night before in the *Evening Herald*, encouraging anyone who sympathised to come along to the protest.[13] As Cathal Kerrigan notes, 'Picketing a garda station was an act of aggression and we really just wanted to stand outside Pearse Street and just say, you know what? Enough is enough and you are not going to push us around anymore.' He continues: 'There was a group of us that was more left, radical and suspicious of the State, and we would have been especially conscious of the gardaí.'[14] This heightened sense of awareness among GDC members, many of whom were also associated with GAI, extended to other organisations like Gays Against H-Block Armagh. These groups frequently took to the streets in protest and, in doing so, gained valuable experience in dealing with intimidating gardaí encounters.

Following the GDC's successful first picket of Pearse Street, a public meeting was held encompassing various groups, including the National Gay Federation (NGF). Eamon Somers, its then president, expressed his concern that 'people are being pressurised specifically because they are gay and asked questions that are not relevant to the crime'.[15] He went on to note that, while the gardaí had promised the NGF that any evidence collected from the gay men that was of no relevance to the investigation would be destroyed, he had reservations as to whether this was truly the case.[16] Concluding his speech, he remarked that the NGF would now start channelling resources into investigating garda practices and procedures in relation to the community through the establishment of a committee comprising political and professional figures. 'People are being forced off of the streets,' he said simply.[17] One individual was reported telling the meeting that he had become privy to the garda files where he saw 'many photographs of people who were gay' and two instances of information on people who were not even in Dublin at the time of Charles Self's murder. The ICCL expressed concern about the records and queried whether they would be destroyed.[18] This meeting and the coverage from the likes of *The Irish Times* brought a significant amount of credibility to the GDC's campaign.

Empowering gay men through consciousness-raising and information activism was crucial, so the GDC developed a leaflet to provide gay men with information about their civic and legal rights. The leaflet noted three core points in particular:

If you are stopped you are not obliged even to give your name and address, but it is usually best to do so.

You need not go to the Garda station unless you are arrested. Even then you should say nothing until you see a solicitor (IGRM and NGF will provide a solicitor for any gay person who needs one).

Do not give fingerprints or allow yourself to be photographed. If you have already made a statement or have been photographed, consult a solicitor immediately. They will advise you of what action to take.[19]

The leaflet was disseminated in various gay spaces and locations across the city, reflecting the GDC's concerted effort to reach as many gay men as possible. As Kerrigan notes, 'We would go into the bars and speak to people and empower them, telling them what to do, giving them leaflets. We were doing the basis of all political activism, kissing babies, going along and looking somebody in the eye and saying, "I have a message, here is a leaflet that will help you and make your life better. If they harass you this is what you do and what you say."'[20]

Following the leaflet distribution campaign to raise awareness among gay men in relation to their rights, a second picket was organised to keep momentum going. The prevailing distrust of the police showed no signs of abating, particularly in light of Jack Marrinan, the general secretary of the Garda Representative Association, making statements to the press such as, 'The values of society had taken a plunge in recent years with people like homosexuals and pro-abortionists demanding rights,' which, he argued, enabled crime to thrive.[21]

Prior to 1982 the Irish gay and lesbian civil rights movement had been finding its feet. There was an emerging scene, with the Hirschfeld Centre providing a necessary and crucial social enclave within Temple Bar, and broader rights-based politics was making some headway. Yet the murder of Charles Self, and the flawed investigation that emerged in its wake, was a significant moment that demonstrated to the gay community how vulnerable they still were. The GDC emerged out of the garda harassment and offered a mode of defence, visibility and leadership. It returned confidence to gay men, showing that they could fight back. The investigation into Charles Self's murder ultimately ceased its harassment of the gay community. Unfortunately, no individual was identified or arrested in connection with the crime, and to this day, it remains an unsolved case.

The GDC played a crucial role in the evolution of the Irish gay and lesbian civil rights movement. It also laid the foundation for the Dublin Gay Collective (later the Dublin Lesbian and Gay Collective), which would become a powerful and alternative voice for the community. This new wave of activism challenged prevailing norms, fought against police harassment and formed robust alliances, particularly with the abortion rights campaign. The GDC, despite its brevity, marked a seminal flashpoint in the broader history of queer rights in Ireland, igniting a movement that would shape the course of Irish history in the years to come.

Later that year, on the evening of 8 September 1982, John Roche, a gay man from Cork City, was found dead in the Munster Hotel where he worked as a night porter.

He had been stabbed in the chest.[22] The man accused of murdering him, Michael O'Connor, stabbed him because he 'accused John Roche of trying to make him gay'.[23] The next day, on 9 September, back in Fairview, Cathal and Máirtín woke up, thankfully, without the presence of gardaí on their doorstep. However, as the morning drew on, they noticed an unusual commotion on their street. Soon word reached them through a housemate who had returned from the local newsagent's: a young man had been brutally beaten to death in Fairview Park, just around the corner at the top of their road. The tragic death of this young man sent shockwaves through the local community, and for everyone at Windsor Avenue, it hit close to home. They all walked in Fairview Park daily. Later that day, the full weight of the tragedy would strike Cathal and Máirtín even harder when they discovered that the victim was Declan Flynn, a fellow gay man from the Dublin scene, who had been fatally attacked in a horrific act of 'queer-bashing'.

Cathal and Máirtín were deeply affected by the grim reality of another gay man's murder, particularly one that had occurred in their own neighbourhood. This tragedy served as an alarming reminder that, as gay men, they remained susceptible to the threat of homophobic violence and assaults. The fact that Declan Flynn's murderers received suspended sentences with no jail time at their trial in 1983 added to the community's distress. In response, those who had been part of the GDC – now transformed into the Dublin Lesbian and Gay Men's Collective – took the lead in organising the

Stop Violence Against Gays and Women protest march to Fairview Park. This demonstration marked one of the earliest and most conspicuous acts of resistance by the LGBTQ+ community in Ireland, often dubbed Ireland's Stonewall moment, and it set in motion a culture of public demonstrations that would grow for years to come.

But these movements and responses emerged out of tragic circumstances. Over the course of 1982, four lives were extinguished in homophobically charged attacks, although the circumstances of the Charles Self case remains unclear to this day. The murders of four men, whether through 'queer-bashing' or the use of a 'gay panic' defence to justify their killing, underscore the stark reality that being gay in 1982 could be unsafe and dangerous. Charles Self. George Leonard. John Roche. Declan Flynn. Let us remember them.

10

'Am I a Qualified-Enough Lesbian?'

*The Belfast Lesbian Line and
Cross-Border Lesbian Solidarity*

In 1988 Rita Wild, from the Bogside in Derry, registered at Queen's University Belfast as a mature student. As she threw herself into student life, she began to realise that she was attracted to women. The problem was, she did not know where to find any lesbians. One day, as she was perusing the Queen's Students' Union newsletter, a small box advertisement at the bottom caught her eye: Belfast Lesbian Line. *That's where the lesbians are*, she said to herself, *sorted!*[1] The following Thursday, Rita went out to a public phone box in the depths of the night to make a call to the Lesbian Line – the only night of the week that it operated. She was a nervous wreck, not knowing where this phone call was going to lead. But the Lesbian Line volunteer quickly realised Rita was a first-time caller. 'Don't worry, you'll be grand,' came the voice.[2] And that's all Rita needed to hear.

As part of its range of services, the Belfast Lesbian Line offered a befriending initiative for newcomers, where two Lesbian Line volunteers would meet a lesbian in a public place during the day in an environment without alcohol. Arranging to meet outside Belfast City Hall that weekend, the Lesbian Line volunteer said to Rita, 'You'll know me because I'll have my bike.' Rita replied, 'And you'll know me because I'll be wearing a red jacket.' The following Saturday, Rita found herself wracked with nerves at the prospect of meeting a 'real-life lesbian'.[3] Approaching City Hall, she saw a bike chained to the front, with high handlebars and a basket. *That looks like a postmistress's bike*, Rita thought to herself, concluding that it had all the trappings of the kind of bike that a lesbian would ride, so she stayed, watching it closely.[4] When no lesbian materialised, Rita began to walk around the corner of City Hall to see if she was elsewhere. And there, holding a racing bike with all the bells and whistles, was Rita's lesbian. She ushered Rita into a new world, teaching her not to make assumptions about lesbians (and lesbian bikes, for that matter). Quickly, Rita threw herself into lesbian life in Belfast and became an activist with the Belfast lesbian community.

The Belfast Lesbian Line came into existence in 1974, originally as part of Cara-Friend, which was Northern Ireland's befriending and information organisation for gay and bisexual men and women. In 1979, Thursday nights became the designated time of the week for Lesbian Line activities.[5] This period also saw a burgeoning gay and lesbian civil rights movement emerge in Northern

Ireland. In 1971, the Gay Liberation Society (GLS) was established at Queen's University Belfast, of which the Belfast Sappho lesbian group became a component and met regularly in the Queen's University Students' Union.[6] Cara-Friend's first annual report contends that Sappho emerged from women who called up the phone line and met through befriending one another.[7] Out of the GLS came the Northern Ireland Gay Rights Association (NIGRA) in 1975, which dedicated itself to the campaign to decriminalise homosexuality.[8] Cara-Friend did receive support through a grant from the Department of Health and Social Services at Stormont in 1975, but 1976 saw the phone line premises and NIGRA being raided by the Royal Ulster Constabulary (RUC), and twenty key members of the organisations being arrested, with 'prosecutions for sodomy set in train by the Northern Ireland Director for Public Prosecutions'. This remained the case until the Attorney General of the British government in London intervened and stopped the prosecution from proceeding.[9]

In the early days of Cara-Friend, it became evident that there was a need to carve out space for women specifically. Many of the callers were lesbians looking to speak with women, rather than gay men, but the men outnumbered the women two to one.[10] As a result, the line received its own rooms for women who wanted to come in and be in a women-designated space. For every phone call received at the Lesbian Line, it was hoped that a befriending, such as the one Rita experienced, would result from it. This was often done through

Lavender Lynx, a fortnightly women-only meeting and the only regular lesbian event in the city at the time.[11] It was an alcohol-free safe space, based at the Carpenter Club, and was especially good for women just coming out on the scene.

The development of the Lesbian Line in Belfast was reflective of a growing lesbian consciousness on the island of Ireland, with the Dublin Lesbian Line being founded by Joni Crone in 1979. In 1985, the Cork Lesbian Line also began operating on Thursday nights and aimed to counteract 'stereotypical images of lesbians' and to tackle the problem of lesbians in isolation.[12] A Galway Lesbian Line was established in 1988 to provide a resource for more rural lesbians across the West of Ireland.[13] All of the Lesbian Lines tried to help women in various ways – to cope in their marriages if they felt trapped, to come out or just by simply being a kind voice on the other end of the phone.

The Belfast Lesbian Line had its own specific experiences. Despite operating on the island of Ireland, the political and cultural climate of Northern Ireland had significant ramifications on the lesbian and gay people there in the 1970s and 1960s. Heather Fleming came of age during this particularly tumultuous time, before becoming a central figure in the Belfast Lesbian Line. Heather was from rural County Down and realised early on that she was different. She sought out a lesbian community for herself in her local library, trying to find some trace of lesbian culture in the indexes of books, until she eventually came across a reference to the Lesbian

Line in the *Belfast Telegraph*.[14] She moved to Belfast the following year to start university and, in 1984, started to volunteer for Lesbian Line, which was struggling: the pool of volunteers was low and there were not enough women to keep the phone line going. In 1982 the line had to be 'cut back to only the third Thursday of each month due to a lack of sufficient volunteers and from June it was completely suspended. In the absence of women on the telephone rota, women callers are spoken to by male befrienders. This we hope will only be a temporary stop-gap solution until more women join the telephone service.'[15] Indeed, this remained the case until more volunteers, of which Heather was one, joined the line, where she grew the volunteers and co-wrote the training programme.

Heather recalls how lesbian and gay culture in Northern Ireland was denounced by the Democratic Unionist Party (DUP) and its leader Ian Paisley, who created an intolerable cultural climate for lesbians and gay men. The introduction of the Sexual Offences Acts 1967 partially decriminalised same-sex activities between men in private spaces by the British, but this did not apply to Northern Ireland and was resisted by unionists.[16] With the liberalisation of the laws in England and the formation of NIGRA in 1975, the DUP launched its 'Save Ulster from Sodomy!' campaign – a 'concerted and persistent campaign, which advertised itself in the newspapers and demonstrations and pamphleteering on street corners'.[17] As Sean Brady describes, in Paisley's world-view Ulster 'had to be made fit for the second coming of Christ and therefore needed "saving" from sodomy'.[18] Homosexuality was eventually decriminalised in 1981 following Jeffrey Dudgeon's campaign in *Dudgeon v United Kingdom*, where the European Court of Human Rights ruled that Northern Ireland did not have the right to impose a total ban on homosexuality. Even with this ruling, the resistance of the DUP and Paisley contributed significantly to a continuing climate of homophobia in Northern Ireland.

The 'Save Ulster from Sodomy!' campaign – which also received support from the Roman Catholic Church – served as a highly visible marker of homophobia that shaped the sexualities of lesbian and gay people in Northern Ireland. As Heather recalls, 'We got calls from lesbians from all over Northern Ireland, people who were isolated in rural areas, people who were affected badly by religion and the homophobia that came from religion and not wanting to be lesbian.'[19] The worst calls for Heather were the women who would phone the line and simply ask, 'How can I change? I don't want to be like this' – all because of their religion and what the likes of the DUP were spreading throughout Northern Ireland.[20] Many thought they would never find a happy life; some were suicidal.

While religiosity was a significant influence, the climate of the Troubles created another layer of complexity for lesbians coming out. Befriending was a core part of the Belfast Lesbian Line's service, but many of the callers were resistant to meeting in Belfast's city centre as a result of the many security checks in place.

During the 1980s, very little in the city centre would have been open from 5 p.m. because of bombings and security risks. The only social place open would have been the Chariot Rooms, Belfast's first gay-run bar, which was in one of Belfast's central gated areas, meaning that any lesbian or gay man looking to go to one of the few queer spaces in Belfast had to go through a military checkpoint.[21] As Heather remembers: 'A female army officer would have body-searched the women going through ... That was never a pleasant experience. Big steel turnstiles. Click, click, click. You couldn't have got in any other way.'[22] Homophobic remarks would be made to suspected gays and lesbians going to the Chariot Rooms by the British Army officials.[23] Marian Duggan recounts a conversation with a gay person living in Northern Ireland, who noted that, 'People were getting shot and tortured and still the police found the time to harass gay people.'[24] This interaction with security checkpoints meant that many of the callers to the Lesbian Line were reluctant to do befriending, preferring to stay as regular callers instead.

Even in the Chariot Rooms, the spectre of the Troubles lurked, dampening the joyful atmosphere. One night Heather was dancing away to her heart's content, the disco beats pulsing through her as she bounced across the floor. Suddenly, the music stopped. The lights went on. It wasn't time to go home, so this meant one of two things: the British Army or the RUC were coming in. (This was a frequent occurrence and a form of State intimidation against the gay and lesbian community.) On this night, it was the RUC, heavily armed. The dance floor split and everyone moved towards the sides as officers walked around staring at each gay and lesbian, brandishing their sub-machine guns. When one RUC officer got to Heather, he looked at her with disgust, hate and anger. She met his gaze and said, 'You know, you don't need all this palaver. If you want to come in here and get yourself a boyfriend, come on in!'[25] Furious, but restraining himself, the RUC officer moved along and the intruders left the building. Heather's outburst came as a result of consistent State intimidation towards the gay and lesbian community. She notes that many of the lesbians who had just come out through befriending with the Lesbian Line would have left the lesbian scene in Belfast or been reluctant to return because of this State intimidation.[26]

Despite these issues, the Belfast Lesbian Line continued its work and the phones rang off the hook every Thursday night. Volunteers noted that the silent calls were the most difficult. Assuming there was a distressed woman at the other end, too afraid to speak, the volunteers would reassure the caller, saying, 'I know how hard it is to talk, here's what we do at Lesbian Line. We are here for befriending, it's in a safe space. You're not alone.'[27] More often than not, calls would end with the voice of a man who was obviously masturbating. These 'wank calls', as they were called, were a frequent disturbance to the Lesbian Line's delivery of service, but the volunteers were conscious that, even though silent calls regularly ended like this, they had to keep going in case there was a woman on the other end of the line who really needed their help.

Claire Hackett came to the Lesbian Line through the women's movement and feminist groups she was part of during her student days at Queen's in the early 1980s. Here she became friends with Heather, who at the time was trying to get the Lesbian Line back off the ground with a solid base of volunteers. Slightly nervous and conscious of her inexperience, Claire thought to herself, *Am I a qualified-enough lesbian to do this?*[28] Despite her reservations about her lesbian credentials, Claire volunteered with the Lesbian Line for the next sixteen years, helping many women who were trapped in their marriages or living in fear of losing custody of their children. Claire noted the many nuances of lesbian experience during this time, from those who would have identified as Catholic working class, to republican lesbian feminists, to Unionist lesbians.[29] While there were forms of sectarianism within the lesbian and gay community in Northern Ireland, as noted by Marie Mulholland, many within the Lesbian Line worked collaboratively, with the simple of aim of building community.[30] Claire emphasises that the Belfast Lesbian Line strove towards connections with the Lesbian Lines in the Republic, highlighting that they considered 'Ireland as our organising unit' and that building lesbian solidarity across the island seemed natural.[31] While the Troubles and religiosity affected 'the people of Northern Ireland by creating a culture in which people were more prejudiced against gay men and lesbians than the rest of the United Kingdom', there was significant queer joy and fun beyond the political violence, sectarianism and homophobia.[32] This community was built by the activists in the Belfast Lesbian Line, particularly through cross-border collaboration.

Social links were significant to promoting fun, and Claire Hackett argues that the Cork Women's Fun Weekend was a crucial social artery that developed connections with the Belfast Lesbian Line, as many of the volunteers travelled down to participate and fell in love.[33] 'Our connections were much stronger with Cork than Dublin and I think that comes down to the Cork Women's Weekend,' she says.[34] The weekend 'aimed to provide a space to recognise and celebrate the identity, culture and community that women were creating'.[35] As Orla Egan notes, it was also a crucial antidote to the politics; it was just about having a good time.[36] From the social links that had emerged, an opportunity arose from Co-operation North, an organisation founded in 1979 as a cross-border reconciliation body, with the aim of advancing 'mutual understanding and respect by promoting practical co-operation between the people of Northern Ireland and the Republic of Ireland'.[37] Co-operation North's establishment ensured that cross-border initiatives would become more suitable and that a 'climate of goodwill' would be fostered between people across the island, along with hopefully encouraging political leaders to 'explore political options which are not open in the present atmosphere'.[38]

In 1988 the Belfast Lesbian Line and the Cork Lesbian Line decided to join together on an application in the hope of funding a cross-border exchange to share resources between the Lesbian Lines, particularly after the success of the National Lesbian Line Conference held in Cork in January 1988. An application by Women's News in Belfast and the Women's Place in Cork had previously been successful under Co-operation North, but this was the first time 'lesbian' was going to be explicitly front and centre of the application. In putting the application together, Rita Wild recalls they knew it 'had to be outstanding. We were pretty sure that they wouldn't want to fund a bunch of lesbians, so we had to work really hard to make sure they couldn't refuse us.'[39] Against all odds, the application ended up becoming successful through the Women's Links programme, the section of the Co-operation North initiative aimed at promoting activities around women's issues, with Heather Fleming noting it was 'a big deal' for lesbians to receive 'official' recognition like this. And so Co-operation North took a chance on a group of lesbian activists in the spirit of exchange and generosity across the border.

On a cold November morning in 1988, Heather Fleming was checking her watch, getting impatient. Standing beside a bus that she had borrowed for the next few weeks from Queen's University Students' Union, she had been left with the task of packing it full of lesbians, and she wanted to get the show on the road. Her comrades threw their luggage on to the back of the bus on the Queen's campus and piled aboard. Heather did a headcount, saw that everyone was

present and hopped onto the bus. As she got into the driver's
seat and put the bus in gear, cheers erupted from the group.
Their destination: across the border of Northern Ireland to
Galway, where the Corkonian and Galwegian lesbians were
eagerly awaiting their arrival. The activists had planned this
exchanges over several months, since being awarded the
funding form Co-operation North, settling on Galway as
the halfway point to meet. And so a bus of lesbians made
their way from Belfast towards Galway, bursting with
joy at the prospect of co-operation, developing alliances
and, most crucially, having fun. As they drove south, the
group changed the words of the Ulster ballad 'The Sash',
which commemorated the victory of King William III in
the Williamite War, to give the song a queer slant. Heather
smiled as she twisted and turned round the sharp bends of
Ireland's country roads, joining with her fellow activists in
singing their own 'lesbianified' rendition:

'For she was young and she was beautiful and
her figure it was fine,
    So I wrapped my arms around her and I asked
her to be mine,
    She said would she would be willingly, so I
kissed her on the lips,
    Wrapped my arms around her shoulders and
my legs around her hips.'

The Lesbian Lines had several aims: consciousness-
raising, resource-sharing and having fun, partying and
romancing at night. The Galway Lesbian Line activists

hosted many of the Cork and Belfast attendees in their homes, packed in together onto sitting-room and bedroom floors to sleep.[40] Much of the work by day centred around workshops, where each groups would discuss how they operated their line and how they handled calls. Claire recalls a concern raised around the age profile of the girls calling, along with how to develop strategies around avoiding activist burnout.[41] Many of the attendees noted that their respective Lesbian Lines had small pools of volunteers and that a lot of pressure was put on a small number of people to keep these crucial resources going long-term: 'We would talk about dilemmas we faced – we were very young to be dealing with them. It was a way of sharing problems and good practice to improve what we were doing. We also exchanged ideas around training. It would have helped the Galway Lesbian Line also, who were just starting.'[42] Some of the anecdotes recounted included one about the telephone operator not knowing how to spell 'lesbian'. There was also discussion about the lack of a sustainable funding stream and support, how to deal with men who called the line and the significant difficulty around placing adverts in local newspapers, all because the word 'lesbian' was mentioned.[43] Counselling and listening skills were also honed during training sessions. Participants were paired with someone unfamiliar and strategies were worked on, with feedback given in a collective and constructive way.[44] The Belfast Lesbian Line later hosted Cork, in 1989, to continue much of the work that had been done. Outside of the work, the fun encompassed ceilidh tunes being played by one of the participants, sean nós singing and other sorts of sing-songs – and in one instance a fire-juggling display.[45] While very much oriented around developing a lesbian consciousness politically, these exchanges were crucial in building lesbian solidarity across the island.

The exchange was so successful that later in 1989 an independent panel of judges awarded first prize to the Belfast and Cork lesbian exchanges in the Women's Links category.[46] The presentation of the awards was usually a public event with significant media presence, to give visibility to the Co-operation North programme. Things were not to be so simple on this occasion, however. As Rita Wild recalls, 'We were told that we were going to receive the award in an antechamber, privately, with no press. This was completely different to the other awardees, who were getting the full bells and whistles in public.'[47]

The story of the Belfast Lesbian Line reveals a less divisive history of Northern Ireland during the Troubles. While the Troubles certainly created a very specific experience for lesbian and gay people in Northern Ireland, communities and groups found ways of making connections, establishing friendships and finding romance outside of political violence and sectarian division. This is not to diminish the context of the Troubles and the effects of religious fundamentalism experienced by many – but it shows that queer life did go on. The work of Heather Fleming and Claire Hackett was indicative of the work of many volunteers with the

Belfast Lesbian Line, as was Belfast lesbian activism via Rita Wild. These women gave their time to help other women out of their closets and find them a community, often in very difficult circumstances. Whether it was talking to them on the phone, befriending them outside City Hall or driving them to events, the Belfast Lesbian Line was a crucial marker and stepping stone for women across Northern Ireland. And you could be certain, if you let yourself, that you would have fun along the way.

11

Pride in Parenting

*Toni Burgess and the Story of
Lesbian and Gay Parenting Rights*

It's a cold Ash Wednesday morning on 28 February 1990 as Toni Burgess stands beside her solicitor in Cobh District Court. She has made the journey from across the harbour, returning to her native coastal town for the first time in several months. Blowing into her hands, trying to warm herself up, she steps nervously from side to side. Her solicitor turns to her, gives her some reassuring words: 'It'll be okay … Should be quick.'[1] Although well-intended, the reassurances do nothing for Toni's nerves, which continue to rack up as the courthouse begins to fill. Behind her, she hears footsteps and, trying not to turn her head too much and give away how nervous she is, she sees her husband and his solicitor take their places in the courtroom. Soon, members of her family, to whom she has not spoken in months, file in. Toni tries to smile and wave at them, but they look coldly through her, ignoring her. The court falls silent and the judge briskly moves towards the bench, taking his seat on a raised platform, looking down on everyone, about to decide Toni's fate. Immediately, Toni's heart drops. The judge has ashes on his forehead. Taking a deep breath, Toni thinks to herself, *Well, I'm fucked. This judge is a middle-aged, heterosexual Catholic.*

Toni was in court that day seeking to maintain custody of her two children.[2] But the odds were against her: she was a lesbian mother who had left her marriage. As the court proceedings began, it became clear that things were not going her way; the judge concluded the trial, giving Toni access to her children at the weekends, but maintaining a custody order with her ex-husband. Devastated, Toni left the courthouse. She was not giving up without a fight, however, and resolved to develop a battle plan to maintain custodial rights over her children.

Toni Burgess's story is similar to those of many other lesbians who, having realised their sexual identities later in life after marriage, had to fight for access to their children. The situation for gay and lesbian parents in Ireland during the latter half of the twentieth century was precarious, especially for lesbian mothers. As Tonie Walsh notes, 'Lesbian mothers were routinely denied access and custody of their children in cases of separation.'[3] Parental rights for gay, and especially lesbian, parents were a central concern of the early gay-rights movements. For Gay Pride Week 1980, campaign literature clearly stated: 'We demand the right for those of us who have children, particularly lesbian women, to have the rights of custody to those children on an equal footing with heterosexual parents.'[4] Consciousness-raising around these issues was especially important. Eamon Somers, who was president of the NGF and had established the Tuesday Talkshop forum in the Hirschfeld Centre, took part in a mini-marathon during the 1980s with Tuesday Talkshop participants, where he sported a T-shirt with the slogan *Gay Dads* as he ran through the streets of Dublin. Eamon's two children proudly watched from side, which was followed by celebrations in the Toby Jug pub on South King Street.[5]

Gay people often experienced enormous difficulty in the wake of a separation from a heterosexual marriage. As the Dublin Lesbian and Gay Men's Collective noted, the trauma involved in coming to terms with one's sexuality can be difficult enough, but for lesbian and gay people who are married, the problems can be even more significant.[6] The Collective state that there are 'particular problems for lesbians who attempt to talk with their husbands about their sexuality. Women are more vulnerable both physically and economically. For those with children, withholding custody or access has often been used as a means of threatening them.'[7] A woman who gained custody of her children in an out-of-court agreement had no guarantee that her husband would stick to it. In addition, lesbian women often settled for any kind of access given by their husbands 'for fear of coming off worse if she goes to court where she will be completely at the mercy of the judge's prejudices'.[8]

Up until the late 1980s, British divorce cases saw six out of ten lesbians losing custody of their children, without any consideration or credence given to the ability of these mothers to care for those children.[9] This was a significant concern for many lesbians across the UK and Ireland married with children throughout the 1970s and 1980s. Pauline O'Donnell was a volunteer with the Dublin Lesbian Line during the 1980s and recalls receiving calls from women who felt trapped in their marriages, too afraid to leave because their lesbian identity would result in them losing custody of their children.[10] Rita Wild recollects a distressing incident in which her lesbian identity was weaponised by a friend's husband during a custody dispute. The husband sought sole custody of their children, portraying Rita's 'lesbianism' as a detrimental influence on his wife's suitability as a mother.[11] Objections to lesbian mothers having access to their children centred around two grossly misinformed positions: that the 'psychopathology' of a lesbian mother 'deviates' from heterosexual mothering and that 'children of lesbian mothers are assumed to fall victim to negative psychosexual developmental influences'.[12] Nancy Polikoff of the Women's Legal Defence Fund in Washington DC in the 1980s noted that the legal system 'is not friendly to lesbians and gay men' and that 'the courtroom is no place in which to affirm our pride in our lesbian sexuality'.[13] For success in maintaining custody, Polikoff states that, 'A lesbian mother must portray herself as [...] the spitting image of her ideal heterosexual counterpart – and preferably asexual. Only then does she stand a chance of retaining custody', with this often taking an enormous toll on a lesbian mother.[14] The situation was even more difficult in Ireland, given that there was 'significant difficulty in obtaining a legal separation', since divorce was illegal and remained so until 1996, which further complicated legal custody situations.[15] Lesbian mothers in the midst of all this saw the odds stacked against them, and people like Toni Burgess had an uphill battle to ensure that they still had access to their children and could be the mothers they wanted to be.

Toni Burgess was born in 1953 in the harbour town of Cobh, County Cork, the youngest of seven children. Having met her husband at 13, she married at 19 in Cobh's St Colman's Cathedral in 1972. Growing up, Toni had no awareness of the existence of lesbian and gay people, apart from two local men whose gay identities were often the target of derisive humour throughout Cobh. Toni's life adhered to conventional expectations, as she followed the traditional path set for women during the 1970s and 1980s. After a year of working in London, she returned to Cobh with her husband, where they bought a house and decided that they wanted to start a family. As time went on, she had a daughter, closely followed by a son. To anyone looking in from the outside, Toni had the perfect life. She had two children she adored, a husband she loved, a family car outside the house and a foreign holiday once a year.[16] Life was as good as it could get for an Irish family during the 1980s.

Toni's life as a homemaker and mother continued, as she dedicated herself to raising her children. Then, on one crisp spring morning, with the sun casting its gentle glow over Cobh's picturesque harbour, she took her little ones for a stroll in the pram, eventually crossing paths with a friend. Amidst the typical exchange of updates and local gossip, their conversation took an interesting turn when Toni's friend mentioned the Quay Co-Op, a co-operative and social haven on Sullivan's Quay in Cork City.[17] In the midst of this casual conversation, Toni's friend remarked how her best friend, a gay man, found the Co-Op to be a welcoming spot for the LGBTQ community. Inexplicably, this snippet of information triggered something within Toni. As she bade her friend farewell and continued her walk, she couldn't shake the sense of being drawn to the Quay Co-Op – a magnetic pull towards a place she had never visited or knew existed. She couldn't quite fathom why this yearning had taken hold, but she felt an undeniable need to explore it and gain a deeper understanding of this mysterious attraction.

The Quay Co-Op opened in May 1982 to 'create a development space [...] and to initiate employment in doing so'.[18] The four-storey building provided a location for the Cork Lesbian Line and Gay Information telephone helpline, along with a base for social justice campaigns, such as the Anti-Amendment Campaign to the Eighth Amendment.[19] The Quay Co-Op became a crucial hotbed for gay and lesbian activism and community-building and established a safe haven for activist and minoritised groups with a range of causes in Cork City.[20]

A few weeks after the chat with her friend, Toni decided to go and see what all the fuss was about at the Quay Co-Op, so she made her way into Cork City one Saturday morning. When she arrived at the threshold of the building, Toni struggled to cross it and paced up and down Sullivan's Quay, along the banks of the River Lee, thinking to herself, *Will I? Won't I? What am I going to find in there when I go in?* After what felt like hours of contemplation, Toni summoned the resolve to step inside. To her surprise, what she encountered was far from the outrageous extravagance she had imagined. The place was nice and welcoming, and the people she observed just seemed a little different, yet she felt an unspoken connection with them. While she did not speak to anyone on that visit, it marked a significant first step on Toni's journey of self-discovery. Witnessing this vibrant lesbian and gay community provided her with a glimpse of her own identity, setting her on the path toward a deeper understanding of who she truly was.

Toni would soon encounter the lesbian and gay community once again, in the most unlikely of places: her local mother-and-baby group. Advertisements from community groups in the city were regularly posted at mother-and-baby groups in surrounding towns and villages. After finishing an exercise class with her daughter, she looked at the notice board and saw an ad for the Other Place, an LGBTQ venue and resource centre in Cork City, which was advertising an event for the following weekend. Thinking that there was a community to find for herself somewhere there, Toni once again made her way into Cork, towards the Other Place on Augustine Street. Walking nervously up the stairs into the event space, Toni looked around and saw a room full of lesbian women. Immediately, she thought to herself, *I'm home*.

As Toni began to come to terms with her true self as a lesbian, she immersed herself in Cork's vibrant lesbian community. Her involvement in this community deepened over time, with evenings spent at Loafers Bar and the Steeple Bar's lesbian events. A pivotal moment occurred during her attendance at the Cork Women's Fun Weekend, when she met someone who would become her partner for a number of years. This encounter compelled her to face a difficult truth: the life she had been leading in Cobh as a contented wife and mother of two was no longer tenable. With a growing sense of anxiety, she steeled herself to have the crucial conversation with her husband, eventually mustering the courage to tell him that she was a lesbian and had to be with the person she loved. She reflects, 'My husband, a good man, was blindsided when I revealed that I was leaving.'[21] From an outsider's perspective, it might have seemed like Toni had it all and was now throwing it all away.

As their separation unfolded, the couple agreed that Toni would be granted custody of the children. This arrangement took an unexpected turn after Toni spent a few days with her girlfriend. Her husband suddenly reneged on their agreement, insisting on weekend visitations instead of full custody. Ultimately, it evolved into a situation where Toni had no choice but to part ways with him without her children. She had to pack her bags and tell her children why she was leaving. She went to live with her girlfriend, her world shattered. And so began her two-year battle to regain custody of her children.

In 1990, Toni set out to find a solicitor, who promptly informed her of the uphill battle ahead. When she decided to take her custody dispute to court, a Guardian ad Litem was appointed to assess the situation and determine the best placement for her children. During their initial encounter in Toni's home, she noticed that the guardian purposefully positioned herself at a distance from her in the living room, leaving Toni to wonder, *Does she think if she gets too close, she will become a lesbian?* The guardian meticulously scrutinised every facet of Toni's life, consulting with her children's schoolteachers who uniformly lauded Toni's exemplary motherhood. Yet, curiously, the guardian refrained from observing Toni's own interactions with her children, despite interviewing them and her ex-husband and observing him with them. Regrettably, the first court case concluded without success, necessitating a second custody battle. As Toni observes, while the courts and the system tended to favour the mother over the father, rightly or wrongly, the case was different for lesbian mothers. The very nature of their sexuality, in the eyes of the court, often rendered them as 'unfit mothers'.[22]

Following her initial court case, Toni reached out to a seasoned barrister who offered strategic counsel: she should bide her time for another twelve months before making her case anew in the Cobh District Court. In addition to this, Toni's solicitor, recognising the need to bolster her chances, advised her to approach her lesbian identity in a way that would be read as 'more respectable' and that she should find a house to live in alone.[23]

In 1991, then, Toni left her shared home with her partner – who understood her decision and agreed to continue the relationship – and sought to secure her own place, a step she believed would fortify her argument to maintain custody. In the run-up to a second court date, Toni was once again assigned a Guardian ad Litem, who ended up being the same woman as the last time. While initially concerned, Toni soon saw the guardian's attitude seemed to have shifted. She could see the determination Toni had to see her children and did not think the fact that she was a lesbian should prevent her maintaining custody. On one of her visits to Toni's house, the guardian, marvelling at her library, asked if she had any lesbian fiction, in the hope that she could open her mind and learn something.

On the day of reckoning, Toni felt hopeful as she made her way up the steps of the Cobh courthouse. But she still had to wait for the final outcome. As she settled into her seat at the front of the courtroom once again, the judge came out, took his seat at the bench and, after the formalities had been gone through, quickly made it clear that Toni was a fit mother and should maintain custody of her children. Toni did not realise the momentous, significant achievement she had just attained. Her solicitor turned to her and exclaimed, 'This is groundbreaking! I don't think any woman has gone through this before and been successful.'

Toni immediately left the courthouse and stood outside her children's school. She was early and had to wait a little bit longer than usual until the school bell rang. At 3 p.m., her children ran out of the building and gave her a hug. As she gathered them into her arms, she told them, 'You're going to get to live with me.'[24] Toni described the moment as a miracle. She was one of the first out and open Irish lesbians to fight successfully to keep custody of her children after leaving a marriage.

While Toni's battle ultimately ended in success, there was a significant cost and a greater burden was placed on her to demonstrate that she was a fit parent, simply because she was a lesbian. From mounting a legal battle that took two years, to completely changing her life and living alone without her partner to ensure greater success in court, Toni's story demonstrates the difficulties and discrimination that faced lesbian parents. As Toni notes, many other lesbian mothers would have refused to have taken the legal route to fight for custody simply because doing so would have risked them being identified publicly as a lesbian.[25] While Toni had faced great difficulties in terms of the legal system and society around her, she had a significant well of support from her new-found lesbian community. Toni's success also meant that she became a beacon for other women who wanted to follow her path and fight for custody, and she helped a number of women who came after her.

Having won her legal battle, Toni lived a happy life raising her two children and later having a third child, and she is now a proud grandmother. Her activism for the community was recognised in May 2018 when she received a Cork LGBT InterAgency Award in recognition of her contribution and for being brave enough to put her head above the parapet and fight for the rights of lesbian mothers.

The significant 'yes' vote in the marriage-equality referendum in 2015 may have suggested a new era of expanded rights and protections for LGBTQ parents who choose to get married. However, the battle for comprehensive parenting rights persists, helped by organisations such as Equality for Children. For same-sex couples, the struggle to secure legal recognition for both parents on a child's birth certificate remains a challenge, leaving some parents and children without any legally recognised ties. Even in the wake of such progress, children born to male parents, children conceived via surrogacy, children born abroad or outside of Ireland, and children conceived using known or anonymous donors continue to be excluded from establishing a legal relationship with both their parents.[26] The quest for full parental rights for LGBTQ individuals and couples endures, revealing the work yet to be done in pursuit of true equality, and can be traced right back to Toni Burgess and those of her generation who fought to ensure that lesbians, and gay people more broadly, could be seen as fit parents who love and raise their children as well as any heterosexual parents.

12

Out at Work?

*Louise Hannon, Transgender
Rights and Employment Equality*

It was the beginning of 2008 and Louise Hannon was sitting at home, looking at job adverts. The Irish economy was collapsing, as the international financial crisis had taken hold, and she was desperately looking for some form of employment. She had recently started working in advertising at a radio station, but with the recession, advertising revenue decreased and the station had to let go a number of staff. For Louise it was a case of last in, first out.

She was furious. She had struggled to find a job after being let go from her previous career and had only just landed the radio gig before finding herself facing the job market once again. During the previous five years she had established a successful career as a business development manager. She had enjoyed the work, built up innumerable contacts and made many friends. Yet her workplace had become toxic, unworkable, unbearable – and all because Louise had come out as transgender and wanted to have her transition and identity as a woman recognised officially by her employer; she wanted to be known as Louise going forward. Conditions became so volatile in terms of her new identity that, on 27 August 2007, she'd found that she was being let go. So, sitting in front of her laptop on 18 January 2008, Louise said to herself *No more*, and she sent an email to the director of the Equality Authority to explain that, under the Employment Equality Act, she had been discriminated against as a trans woman. Louise was about to become the first transgender person in Ireland to win a workplace discrimination case.[1]

Employment rights for LGBTQ people in Ireland have always been a contentious site of discriminatory practice. Derek Byrne, having come out in 1985, ventured into the emerging gay scene shortly thereafter. A visit to the Viking gay bar set off a chain of events, when some colleagues spotted him there. Although Derek's colleagues were welcoming and accepting of his presence in a gay bar, news about his attendance and his identity as gay swiftly reached his line manager. One Friday soon after this, Derek was called into his manager's office and unceremoniously told that he was being 'let go' because of issues with his productivity and his work.[2] These issues had never been flagged to Derek, and the company had not followed the usual procedure around dismissal. In the face of this overtly unfair practice, Derek simply said 'no' and started to mount a battle against his employer, as his colleagues told him to ring the union. Derek suspected he was at the hands of a homophobic line manager, but that manager had never explicitly told Derek he was being fired for being gay. The workers took a strike vote, and Derek quickly told members of the National Gay Federation (NGF), who provided him with a solicitor and rallied to his side, with the organisation calling his employer to threaten a picket at the gates of his workplace if he was fired, promising they would bring much negative media attention. Following these threats from the gay community and the solidarity from his colleagues, Derek was called into the office again the following Friday and told that he could have his job back. While Derek suspected that the reason behind letting him go was that he was gay, he was not totally sure. However, Derek's perspective changed when, after the discussion with his line manager, he was on the verge of leaving the office and his manager remarked, 'If you want to wear a blouse, that's okay.'[3] The significance of the blouse was obvious to Derek: it was the mandatory attire for women in the office. Derek now knew that his imminent unemployment had been a result of homophobic management decisions. Only for Derek's defiance and the support from the confident and robust gay community organisation and his colleagues, he could have faced unemployment on the basis of his sexual identity.

These discriminatory practices were also evident in the very public case of Donna McAnallen. In 1993, Donna, a lesbian from Belfast, was working in the Brookfield Holiday Village in Cork City as a lifeguard and fitness instructor. On 26 April of that year, Donna was told by management that she was being dismissed from her job following allegations that she had been seen kissing another woman in the changing rooms.[4] In addition, her supervisor made it clear that Donna was being fired on the basis of her sexuality, telling her that 'having a lesbian working at the fitness club would ruin its reputation'.[5] Donna, furious at the course of events, brought a case to the Labour Court under the Employment Equality Act 1977. Specifically, the act notes 'that discrimination shall be taken to occur ... where by reason of their sex a person is treated less favourably than a person of the other sex'.[6] As Orla Egan notes, a judgement delivered in February 1994 found that 'the worker was treated in an arbitrary and unfair manner' but that this treatment was not covered under the 1977 act, as sexual orientation was not a protected category. The story of Donna's dismissal created a furore across the national media, including her native city's *Belfast Telegraph*.[7] The Labour Court's ruling essentially highlighted the fact that there were no protections in place for workers who were lesbian or gay. McAnallen noted herself that she was aware of the gap in the law and that the case would 'fall on its arse' – but that was not the point. The purpose was to bring attention to the gap in legislation. In response to this, a group called the Friends of Donna McAnallen came together to protest the decision by having coffee in the Brookfield Leisure Complex with T-shirts declaring *I wish I'd kissed Donna McAnallen*.[8] The case of Donna McAnallen put lesbian and gay workers' rights on the political agenda, with the then Minister for Equality Mervyn Taylor committing to changing the act to be more inclusive. Eventually, the Employment Equality Act 1998 was introduced, which gave nine grounds on which discrimination was outlawed, including gender and sexual orientation.

However, even with the welcome progressions brought by the new act, acute forms of discrimination were embedded in the bill. Section 37 of the Employment Equality Act 1998 explicitly permitted discrimination in order to protect the ethos of a religious, educational or medical institution that is under the direction or control of a body established for religious purpose and 'gives more favourable treatment, on the religion ground, to an employee or a prospective employee over that person where it is reasonable to do so in order to maintain the religious ethos of the institution'.[9] Prior to the bill being passed, the Gay and Lesbian Equality Network (GLEN) and the Irish National Teachers' Organisation called for changes to Section 37, with Minister Mervyn Taylor noting he was open to change.[10] Despite these protests, the bill was passed. It was later referred to the Supreme Court for review by President Mary Robinson, who upheld Section 37, meaning that Church-run institutions could actively discriminate on the basis of sexuality.[11] The existence of Section 37 remained a cause of concern for LGBT teachers, who were unwilling to be open about their sexuality within the school community.[12] As one teacher noted, 'The law is saying you mustn't discriminate against gay people – unless you are at a

school or a hospital ... then it's okay? How is that fair?'
As another LGBT teacher noted, they were afraid to
confront issues relating to homophobia within their
classes 'because doing so may have brought unwanted
attention to themselves and their personal lives'.[13]
Section 37 would hang over LGBT teachers for many
years until the Irish government later made it illegal
for religious-run schools to discriminate against LGBT
teachers on the basis of their sexuality.

Despite the problematic emergence of Section 37,
the case of Donna McAnallen, while unsuccessful in
1994, did lay the groundwork for those who came after,
such as Louise Hannon, to take cases on the grounds of
discrimination.

Born in 1948, Louise Hannon was raised near
Belfast as an only child. At a young age, she realised
she felt different when she dressed up in her mother's
clothes. However, one day her mother found her and
reacted extremely negatively. This was a sign for Louise
that gender transgressions needed to be kept to herself,
so for most of the following years, she conformed to
trying to be a boy.[14] As she came into her twenties, her
father fell ill, so she left college to look after the family
farm and, during this period, met her wife, got married
and had two children. One day, in the midst of her time
raising her family, Louise was perusing the now-defunct
News of World and saw April Ashley on the front page.
During the 1950s and 1960s, April Ashley had been a
model, based in England, and had appeared in *Vogue*,
but was later outed by the *Sunday People* tabloid as a

transgender woman. The reveal resulted in her becoming the face of trans hysteria across British media in 1971.[15] Having seen how April Ashley was treated, Louise continued to shy away from her gender identity. At this time, she felt:, 'I don't want to be like that, I don't want to be treated like that.'[16]

Over time, Louise's life changed. Her marriage ended and she decided to move to Dublin for work. In the years leading up to this, she had started to go to counselling with the aim of becoming more comfortable with her transgender identity. Once in Dublin, she began to test the waters, attending the Gemini Club, which had been founded by a woman called Natalie. Gemini was a club for trans people who, after paying a fee, could use the premises for putting on clothes and make-up. It had a core membership of about five hundred. The venue had a main club room and a beauty salon and provided a social outlet for Ireland's trans and gender-diverse community.[17] Through using the Gemini Club, Louise began to gain more confidence around being a transgender woman, leading to her decision to attend the endocrine clinic at St Colmcille's hospital in Loughlinstown, which had been providing a gender service since it started in 2002. Following a series of consultations with Dr James Kelly, Louise made the decision to start hormone therapy. By this time she had established herself within the Irish transgender community, running a trans event on Friday nights in one of Dublin's then premier gay night clubs, The Dragon, from 2004–7.[18]

In October 2006, Louise approached her manager and told him that she was a transgender woman and that she did not think it was possible for her to continue in her role if she were to fully transition in the workplace. She was therefore handing in her notice to resign the following May. The director asked her to reconsider, adding that he felt the workplace could be made inclusive and safe for Louise as she went through her transition. He asked her to consult with her operations manager further on the matter, so Louise proceeded to do so as the operations manager assured her of his support, telling her that he would inform the office staff that November. At this point, Louise felt sheer relief – she was finally going to fully come out and be accepted in the workplace. However, despite an initially supportive reception from her colleagues, things shifted slightly for Louise that December. When she inquired about transitioning at work and starting to present as Louise, her operations manager asked her to postpone things for a few months, as a new staff member would be joining and they wanted this person to become 'settled' first.[19] Despite this small setback, Louise started hormone treatment in February 2007, and on 5 March she was scheduled to change her name legally by deed poll. On the day following her name change, Louise had agreed with her manager that she would arrive in the office in her true gender identity.

The next day Louise went into the office, ready to begin a new phase in her professional career. She was greeted by colleagues, used the female bathroom, made herself a coffee and got to work. When she saw her manager later that morning, she asked for a new email address to reflect her name change. The manager beckoned her into an office and shut the door behind him. Red-faced, he turned to Louise and asked her if she would make her sales over the phone in male form. *But what about everything we discussed over the last few weeks?* she thought to herself. He then continued, 'If there is a need to meet a client in person, I can do it.'[20] He concluded by telling Louise that she may have to continue working using her male identity until Christmas. Louise was shocked and stunned into silence.

A week or so after this conversation, Louise was felled by a bad dose of flu and had to take a number of days off. The day she returned to the office, her manager called her in, raising concerns about her productivity, which Louise attempted to defend. He then asked her to revert to her male identity for the next three months, with Louise protesting that she found this very difficult to comply with. Furious, she called the company's director, informing him that she simply could not revert to her previous identity. She received assurances that she could still come into the office as Louise. However, despite these assurances, she encountered further obstacles when she was told that she was not allowed to use the female toilets, that she could only dress as Louise in the office and that she had to assume her male identity when meeting clients face to face.

She reluctantly agreed to do so, then she was eventually asked to work from home until a new office space was ready, where she would be accommodated on all fronts. What was meant to be only one month of working from home expanded to four months, which took a severe toll on her mental health: 'Eventually, I couldn't take it any longer … I was sitting at home looking at a blue wall with two windows on either side of it and I was losing contact with my colleagues and the world.'[21] Louise's role in sales required an office presence – not being able to go in put her at a disadvantage in terms of building leads. As a result, her productivity was questioned again, adding pressure to acquire new clients. Additionally, IT was slow in processing her email changeover request, which she had request a number of months earlier, in March.

Louise's professional life became essentially unworkable. Having raised these concerns with her company director several times via email, in a meeting that July he simply informed her that she was free to seek alternative employment if she wanted to. Louise was eventually asked to hand in her notice in August 2007. Her transition in the workplace had served to isolate her and she was forced to find another job – a challenging feat in the light of the financial crash, when job opportunities became scarce. And so, in January 2008, five months after leaving her employer of five years, she sent an email to the Equality Authority and set in motion a case that would begin to set things right, or at least confront the transphobia and discrimination she had experienced in the workplace. It would be a number of years before Louise's case would be heard, so in the intervening period Louise prepared her case with her legal team, while trying to live as normal a life as possible and build a career for herself once again.

On 16 September 2010, Louise finally confronted her former employer, First Direct Logistics Limited. That morning, she got dressed, had a coffee, looked in the mirror and assured herself she could do this. She set off on her journey to the Equality Tribunal on Clonmel Street in Dublin, where she met her representative, Siobhán Phelan, before her case began proceedings. Louise relived and rehashed a difficult year in her life.[22] The equality officer concluded through the evidence presented that there was no business need for Louise to work from home and this was essentially a 'way out for the respondent who did not want to deal with the complainant who was now presenting herself as female. I find such an approach constitutes discrimination on both gender and disability grounds.'[23] In particular, the judgment found that it was 'ludicrous' for Louise to manage her transgender identity on particular days and then not on others and that the difficulties regarding Louise's gender lay entirely at the door of her employer – it was a management matter to deal with staff concerns and such issues should not have been Louise's burden to bear. The final judgment ruled in Louise's favour, awarding her seventy-nine weeks of salary to the value of €35,422.71.[24] Louise walked out of the tribunal that day as the first transgender person in Ireland to have a case for discrimination recognised by the Equality Tribunal.

The findings of the case were remarkable in this regard, but what was particularly potent about Louise winning the case was that it established a precedent in case law that transgender identities would be safeguarded under the Employment Equality Act, protecting transgender and gender-diverse people in the workplace. As Louise notes, 'While I took the case for many reasons, it was also my way of putting trans employees and their rights on the agenda. I did not want them to go through what I went through and I wanted employers to take note and get the right policies in place.'[25] The case also garnered a significant amount of media visibility in Ireland and further afield and put trans rights on the political agenda. Her case even made it into the US LGBT outlet *The Advocate*. Louise continued her activism, serving on the board of the Transgender Equality Network of Ireland (TENI) and as a representative within Labour LGBTQ+.

Louise's case was a significant stepping stone in the progress of trans rights in Ireland, adding to the mounting pressure being put on the Irish government around recognising trans rights. The visibility of and conversation around trans rights had emerged into the public sphere with Dr Lydia Foy's legal battle against the Irish State, starting in 1997 and continuing until 2007, just before Louise was about to start her own case with the Equality Authority. Lydia had sought to have her birth certificate reflect her identity as a woman. While this had been refused on several occasions by the Registrar General, Lydia mounted a series of proceedings in the High Court to obtain gender recognition on her birth certificate and, in October 2007, the High Court finally made a judgment and declared that Irish law was incompatible with the European Convention on Human Rights in her case.[26] During those ten years when Lydia mounted her case against the State, several trans activist organisations sprang up to put further pressure on the Irish government. One such group was TENI, which was founded in Cork in 2004 and supported Lydia's case by keeping trans rights on the Irish government's agenda. In 2009, the government committed to introducing some form of gender recognition legislation, with the Gender Recognition Advisory Group being formally established in 2010.[27] Both Louise and Lydia in their legal cases represent the power of public-interest litigation in harnessing and utilising the law to bring visibility to a vulnerable minority and highlight their lack of rights. The battle Lydia Foy had begun in earnest almost twenty years earlier ended in July 2015, when the Gender Recognition Act was passed, enabling Irish citizens to self-determine their gender on official government documents.

Despite the success of Louise's case, the results of a survey conducted by TENI in 2017 found that 55 per cent of transgender and gender-diverse people experienced problems at work, which included unfair dismissal, the denial of a promotion and discrimination based on their gender identity.[28] Trans and gender-diverse people still have to manage the burden of getting their workplaces to recognise their identities in several ways, such as ensuring that internal systems, emails and administrative functions in general align with their chosen names.[29] There is still much work to do to ensure transgender and gender-diverse people are protected to be themselves at work, and in society more broadly, but the brave activism of people such as Louise Hannon has contributed towards making Ireland more inclusive for gender-diverse people, particularly around employment law. Today, Louise is enjoying her retirement. Looking back, she does not see her case as a story of the human spirit triumphing over adversity, but rather as 'a way of making things better for the transgender people coming behind. If what I did, did anything, it was to at least make life easier for the trans community and wake Irish employers up to our reality.'[30]

13

Indecent and Most Obscene

Censorship and Suppression in Queer Irish Culture

As a young woman in secondary school in Ireland during the 1960s, Terri Blanche realised that she was attracted to other girls. The growing realisation of her lesbianism filled her with an innate sense of loneliness. In 1970, at the age of 16, she had nowhere to come out to, but she felt that she needed to express who she was in some way. She also had no idea what it meant to be a lesbian. She had no social spaces to go to. No role models to talk to. These factors coalesced into a very lonely time for Terri, which led to her to find some reflection of her desire and feelings in the culture around her. Eventually, in a feminist pamphlet, she discovered the existence of *The Well of Loneliness* by Radclyffe Hall, published in Britain in 1928. The pamphlet framed the work as a lesbian novel, which immediately resonated with Terri.

The following Saturday she made the journey from Finglas into Dublin's city centre to a bookshop on Nassau Street. Taking deep breaths, she walked up and down the street, trying to muster the courage to go in, until she eventually entered the shop, admitted defeat, walked out and returned home. For much of the following week Terri kicked herself and vowed that she would return and buy Hall's novel. The next time she was in town, Terri built up the confidence to go up to a member of staff and nervously ask, 'I'm so sorry, but have you got *The Well of Loneliness* in stock?' The bookseller looked Terri up and down and replied, 'We don't sell those type of books.' In that moment, Terri felt an utter sense of shame. The bookseller knew why she wanted the book, she knew what Terri was, and she shamed her for that very fact.[1]

The Well of Loneliness was banned by the Censorship of Publications Board in 1929 for its portrayal of desire between women. It remained banned until 1967, and by the time Terri came to look for it in 1970, it had become inexorably entangled in discourses of shame and stigma. Terri's story reflects a number of ways in which official State bodies, along with more local forms of gatekeeping in bookshops, attempted to regulate and govern how queer culture emerged in literature, film and society more broadly.

The introduction of the Censorship of Publications Act in 1929 resulted from pressure by Catholic action groups following Irish independence as a part of a process of 'Catholicisation'.[2] The terms of the act decreed that the Minister for Justice would appoint five individuals to the Censorship of Publications Board, who would then recommend to the minister the permanent prohibition of any book or periodical deemed to be 'in its general tendency indecent or obscene'.[3] 'Obscene' was not clearly defined, whereas 'indecent' was termed 'suggestive of, or inciting to sexual immorality or unnatural vice or likely in any other similar way to corrupt or deprave'.[4] Over the course of the mid twentieth century, the board was regularly criticised – in particular, during a Seanad debate in 1942, when a motion of no confidence was proposed and ultimately defeated. Years later, the Censorship of Publications Act, 1967 limited the period of prohibition of books to twelve years, which allowed the sale of some previously banned books.[5]

While *The Well of Loneliness* was one of the first novels subjected to a ban in Ireland, this apparatus of literary censorship served as the basis of morality campaigns in the early days of the Irish State, especially in relation to diverse sexual and gender representations in literature. In 1941, for example, Kate O'Brien's *The Land of Spices*, a novel about convent life in the Irish countryside and the relationship between a mother superior, Helen, and her student, Anna, was subjected to prohibition under the Censorship Board for the inclusion of 'an oblique reference to homosexuality'.[6] The reference in question was to a single line only, when Helen recounts her discovery of her father's sexuality: 'she saw Etienne and her father in the embrace of love'.[7] The banning of the novel on the basis of this one line indicates the moral morality at play at the heart of the Irish State during this period, which sought to consolidate 'normative' ideas around sexuality. Later, in 1961, John Broderick's novel *The Pilgrimage* was subjected to censorship, as Julia Glyn, the novel's central protagonist, comes to the realisation that her bedridden husband Michael is gay.[8] Patricia Highsmith's novel *Carol* (published at the time as *The Price of Salt* under the pseudonym Claire Morgan), which had been on sale in Ireland for seven years, was banned in 1959 for the explicit lesbian romance between protagonists Therese Belivet and Carol Aird.

Other banned books that demonstrate the prejudices that confronted queer culture in Ireland included *The Gay World* (1968) by Martin Hoffman, *Male Homosexuals: Their Problems and Adaptions* (1974) by Martin S. Weinberg and *The Lesbian Body* (1973) by Monique Wittig.[9] The Censorship of Publications Board regularly attempted to govern matters of sexual 'purity', particularly in relation to lesbian and gay sexuality. In the early 1980s, for example, *Gay News* was the UK's primary LGBTQ magazine and had been in circulation in Ireland since the mid 1970s, primarily through subscription services and sporadic appearances on shelves in newsagents' across the country. Despite this, in February 1982, Cork customs impounded copies of the paper. Subsequently, its distribution in Ireland was forbidden as a result of the Offences Against the Person Act, 1861 and the Criminal Law Amendment Act, 1885, which criminalised gay sexual acts. In an official letter to Robert Palmer of *Gay News* in August 1982, the Office of Censorship of Publications stated that 'the whole tenor of the periodical is indecent and obscene and relates to the crimes of buggery, which is contrary to the Offences Against the Person Act, 1861, Sections 61 and 62, and Gross Indecency between males contrary to the Criminal Law Amendment Act'.[10]

One of the more egregious examples of censorship around gay lives occurred in in 1990, when the children's book *Jenny Lives with Eric and Martin* was banned in Ireland by the Censorship of Publications Board on the grounds of being 'indecent or obscene'. This sparked much resistance from the Irish gay and lesbian civil rights movement. The book follows the life of little Jenny, who is being brought up by her gay father, Martin, and his gay partner, Eric, featuring simple vocabulary and pictures aimed at six to eight year olds. Jenny's mother lives nearby and coparents with her father, and much of the book encompasses banal domesticity: Jenny preparing for Eric's birthday in the back garden with a picnic, annoying her father to get out of bed to make breakfast and accompanying her two fathers to the launderette. The book does cover themes of homophobia when Eric and Martin, on one of their domestic errands, receive homophobic comments from their neighbour Mrs Andrews, with this serving as a learning moment for Jenny, in that people fear what they do not understand. The book started life as *Mette bor hos Morten og Erik*, published in Copenhagen at the beginning of 1982 by author Susanne Bösche and photographer Andreas Hansen. It was published as *Jenny Lives with Eric and Martin* by the Gay Men's Press in London in 1983 and was in circulation and on sale in Ireland from then until 1990.[11] Its censorship in Ireland can be attributed to the furore caused by the book in the UK, which resulted in a targeted campaign and moral panic.

The publication of *Jenny Lives with Eric and Martin* went largely unremarked until 1986, when it was reported that the book was in circulation among Inner London Education Authority (ILEA) primary schools. Calls from parents mounted, claiming that the book was inappropriate for young children; yet in North London, Haringey Education Authority refused to remove the book, leading to a number of parents withdrawing their children from a particular school in protest.[12] The British Secretary of State for Education, Kenneth Baker, demanded that the book be withdrawn from ILEA's central loan collection, and Minister for Arts Richard Luce also called for the book to be removed, describing it as 'intolerant, lunatic and harmful' and stating that such books were a blatant attempt to 'indoctrinate children'.[13] The outcry against the book generally focused on the vulnerability of children and that it would potentially promote 'homosexual lifestyles' to primary-school children as 'normal'. The moral panic that emerged around the book in the public and the political spheres resulted in Margaret Thatcher's Conservative government introducing Section 28 of the Local Government Act 1988, which stated that a local authority 'shall not intentionally promote homosexuality or publish material with the intention of promoting homosexuality' or 'promote the teaching in any maintained school of the acceptability of homosexuality as a pretended family relationship'. Section 28 would remain until it was repealed in 2013.

The targeted campaign and moral panic evident in the UK was similarly harnessed as an opportunity by right-wing groups in Ireland, including Family Solidarity, who claimed that the book was 'totally unchristian and unsuitable for children' and was 'aimed at indoctrinating and corrupting small children'.[14] Following the hysteric approach of the British government, the Censorship of Publications Board decided to ban *Jenny Lives with Eric and Martin* in August 1990. The National Gay Federation (NGF) protested the decision, noting that the book was not sensational in its depiction of a broader version of the family unit, and that its banning sent a clear message to Irish gay and lesbian people that it would be inappropriate for them to form families of their own.[15] Kieran Rose of GLEN called the ban on representing two gay men living together and raising a child a 'fundamental attack on our right to exist socially'[16] – that what was being suppressed was the *idea* that gay men could parent a child. The ban resulted in calls from the community and some gay and lesbian civil rights groups for *Gay Community News* to publish the text of *Jenny Lives with Eric and Martin*. However, after some consideration, the paper decided not to, releasing a statement: 'On taking legal advice, we believe that publication of the text could put our paper at risk as a Family Solidarity representative has stated on radio recently that she would like to see our paper declared illegal as well.'[17] The campaign against and banning of the children's book stood in stark contrast to inciteful material distributed by Family Solidarity a month earlier: their booklet *The Homosexual Challenge* claimed that gay people 'engendered a pool of infection and disease'.[18]

While the Censorship of Publications Board played a significant role in the regulation of how lesbian and gay identities emerged in print and across literature, other apparatuses of the State, along with reactionary resistance from right-wing social actors, were deployed to suppress the emergence of queer visibility in culture. One such instance was the case of *Outwaves*, Ireland's first lesbian and gay radio series based on the community station Horizon Radio, with Family Solidarity threatening to take a legal route to ban the station.[19] Soon after the programme began to broadcast, in 1990, the Council of Social Concern wrote to advertisers on Horizon warning of the consequences of supporting the station and the show, urging them to force the station to stop transmitting the lesbian and gay programme. The letter accused the station of 'actively supporting the very politicised homosexual lobby' and of submitting 'listeners of all ages, especially teenagers, to homosexual propaganda' and saying the programme was 'most unhealthy and abnormal'.[20]

Conservative gatekeepers were also busy silencing other cultural media, as was the case with *Identity* magazine, Ireland's first gay and lesbian literary journal, produced by the NGF and aimed at commercial sale. When the NGF sought to distribute the publication through bookshops in 1981, some stores refused to do so because lesbian and gay people appeared on the cover. The censoring of issues relating to the gay and lesbian community also took place during the AIDS crisis. In 1987 *The Nationalist and Leinster Times*, which was the printing press for *OUT* magazine – at the time Ireland's only indigenous gay publication on commercial sale – disrupted its production due to what it considered to be objectionable content. Gay Health Action (GHA), an activist group responding to the AIDS crisis, had produced a 'safer sex' advertisement to be placed on the back cover of *OUT*'s fourteenth issue. The image and the accompanying text resulted in the printers refusing to produce the advert, as 'some of the material would give offence to their customers'.[21] This delayed the magazine's production, and the team behind *OUT* had to find a new printing press. Similarly, in 1986 GHA submitted a small box advertisement to the *RTÉ Guide* headed 'Aid to fight AIDS', which was rejected by the magazine.[22] Commenting on the refusal to include the advert, RTÉ sales controller Peadar Pierce stated that RTÉ had nothing against the 'terrible problem of AIDS', but 'homosexuality in this country is still illegal and putting it in a family magazine like the *RTÉ Guide* would seem to be giving the whole question of gays some normality, putting it in as if it were a normal situation'.[23] While LGBTQ content had been circulating on RTÉ since 1974, individual controllers of programming and production within the broadcaster attempted to use the criminal laws as a means of censoring and objecting to content. In May 1992, when the Terrence Higgins Trust in the UK released *The Gay Men's Guide to Safer Sex* on VHS, Virgin Megastore Dublin was willing to retail the video, which provided crucial public health information for gay men around safe sex, but were unwilling to do so without a certificate from the Film Censor's Office. Despite the video's immediate public health and education benefits, the release of the video was 'stymied by bureaucratic red tape and fears of financial loss and legal action'.[24]

Later, in 1993, the Health Promotion Unit of the Department of Health compiled a series of advertisements to highlight the dangers of AIDS following the diagnoses of 'almost 1,360 people as HIV positive'.[25] RTÉ refused to broadcast the submitted advertisements, which were meant to air on National AIDS Day on 28 May, taking exception to 'some of the language used' about condoms and the overt sexual representation of gay men. The stance taken by RTÉ on the issue resulted in a response from Michael D. Higgins, who was then Minister for Arts, Culture and the Gaeltacht. He warned in no uncertain terms that he was 'prepared to order RTÉ to broadcast the campaign'.[26] This intervention led to the Department of Health and RTÉ 'amicably resolving the controversy'.[27] While the efforts at censure were circumvented in this instance, it shows how reactionary resistance attempted to use the language of family values and child protectionism, along with the weaponisation of parental morality, to maintain inequalities and suppress public health information for the gay community, especially when, at this point, many gay Irish men had died from AIDS-related illnesses.

Over the course of the twentieth century, censorship by the Irish State and cultural censorship in more unofficial forms, such as pressure from unrepresentative minorities, attempted to suppress how LGBT lives appeared in Irish culture. Moral morality, State-sanctioned 'purity' and the language of family values have striven time and again to engineer or stoke reactionary concern around the existence of LGBT people in culture. While this was aided by the criminal laws in place at the time, the culture of censorship in twentieth-century Ireland provides insights into how LGBT existence was at odds with the State. Additionally, LGBT lives were subjected to what might now be referred to as 'cancel culture' practices today, with attempts made by Family Solidarity and other right-wing groups to de-platform queer culture from the public realm.

The power of these conservative groups brings us back to Terri Blanche, who sought to buy *The Well of Loneliness* and find lesbian representation somewhere in the culture around her. How different might Terri's coming out have been had the forces of conservative Ireland not had their hand on the levers of power? Had she been able to buy *The Well of Loneliness* or *Carol* (*The Price of Salt*), she might have found some positive affirmation to help her on her way. Despite these initial obstacles, however, Terri did eventually come out and became a prominent lesbian activist within the first Irish gay civil rights group, the IGRM. When she could not find resources for lesbianism in the bookshop all those years ago, she set herself up as one, becoming a shining light to guide many others out of the closet and affirm to them that they were lesbian, there was a community, and they would be just fine.

14

Beyond Convention

*Alternative Miss Ireland's
Trailblazing Odyssey (1987–2012)*

'*Alternative Miss Ireland is more than an event,
it's a state of mind where the freaks rule and all
quotidian concerns are banished for one glorious
night of fantastical fun.*' —Lurleen, Alternative
Miss Ireland IX Judge[1]

It's April 2002 and Davina Devine has just come off
the phone to her friend from Outwest, a voluntary
support group for the LGBT community in Ballina,
County Mayo, who has just asked her to do a drag gig.
Davina has never done drag before but, despite initial
reservations, she said to herself, *You know what? This
could be fun.* And so Davina set out for Mayo, dipping
her toes in an unknown world.

Calling herself 'Miss Davina Devine', she created a
new persona and performed in drag for the first time
in glamorous Ballina. The crowd took notice, she was
invited to perform a paid gig in Limerick, and Davina's

drag career began to take off. She entered the Miss Unprofessional Drag competition as part of Dublin Pride festivities that summer of 2002 where she met April Showers. April told her about a drag event and competition, referred to as 'Gay Christmas': 'It happens the Sunday before every Patrick's Day – Alternative Miss Ireland,' she enthusiastically told Davina. Despite being green and naive in the world of drag, Davina agreed to join April, creating a dynamic duo that would enter the ninth Alternative Miss Ireland (AMI) contest set to take place in March 2003.

As AMI IX on St Patrick's Day at the Olympia Theatre quickly approached, Davina and April set about developing their concept and look, harnessing the recent success of Kylie Minogue's *Fever* album to inform their aesthetic. Kylie's *Fever* showcased a bold style, featuring vibrant colours, while presenting a fusion of retro and contemporary visuals, reflecting both disco-era glamour and a contemporary pop sensibility. Despite last-minute costume disasters, with a designer gone incognito, the pair had pulled some green, orange and white looks together for their daywear, eveningwear and swimwear rounds. Opening with B*Witched's 'C'est la Vie', the two set the tone for the night with their high-energy number, followed by what that year's judge Lurleen referred to as 'a leggy drag queen who led the crowd through a Kylie Minogue sing-a-long'.[2] While winning the crown and title of Queen of Ireland eluded them, Davina's journey from Ballina a little over a year earlier struck her: 'Just to be onstage at the Olympia, I mean I had performed on beer crates in Galway and here I was in the Olympia, one of Ireland's biggest stages, as this young drag queen. What an opportunity, and I just felt like a chancer.'³

The impact of AMI became clear to Davina the very next day when her phone started to ping with messages saying, 'You're in the *Evening Herald*!' Davina ran out to get a paper from her local shop, delighted to see her Olympia début splashed across page three. Suddenly, she was hit by a sudden realisation: her grandad religiously read the *Herald*. And Davina was not out as gay. Terrified he might recognise her, she sprinted to his house, only to find him at the table with the *Herald* right in front of him. She chatted manically in an attempt to distract him while, licking his fingers, he parsed the front pages, glancing over page two, with his gaze falling upon page three. Sweat began to drip down Davina's forehead as his gaze remained on the picture of her for what felt like a lifetime, before he turned the page over and continued reading. Her drag persona and shenanigans on the AMI stage at the Olympia were safe for now.

The AMI competition was crucial for allowing participants, especially new and emerging ones, such as Davina, to showcase their creativity, self-expression and talent in a welcoming and affirming environment. It contributed to the growing visibility of Ireland's queer community and was the kickstart to the careers of so many performers. But, crucially, AMI was a form of artistic expression that was also an enclave of queer joy and fun for twenty-five years.

AMI's structure was modelled on Andrew Logan's Alternative Miss World competition, with its daywear, eveningwear and swimwear components, and the judging panel would evaluate the contestants over the course of each stage based on a variety of criteria. Audience interaction became a crucial factor over the course of AMI's history, with text voting being incorporated into the competition as early as 2002. Significantly, the contest was open to any person, thing or animal, the latter of which was truly tested when in 1996 cabaret performer Agnes Bernelle's dog took part – as Miss Dog. In addition to the open entry, the competition was open to interpretation and had no strict dress code, although most entrants tended to play with gender through drag and cross-dressing. As Panti Bliss says, 'AMI is so much more glamorous than the Rose of Tralee, more performance-enhanced than Miss World and just as bizarre as Housewife of the Year.'[4] Contestants were awarded points for poise, personality and originality and for 'transgressing beauty and inventing new desires', with the winner being awarded a Medusa crown of shamrocks.

AMI would serve to challenge the prevailing cultural norms around gender, sexuality, ethnicity and human identity. AMI gave a platform for alternative and queer culture to emerge and explode every year, all the while developing a pipeline of queer talent that would erupt into the mainstream. While the contest grew, venues changed and talent blossomed, the annual event became known as 'Gay Christmas'. What Riverdance did for demonstrating Ireland as a postmodern and 'new' liberal enclave, AMI did for queer Irish culture, which would 'rise as a transgressive firebrand at the Olympia Theatre', becoming a national force.[5]

The origins of this trailblazing odyssey go all the way back to 1 April 1987. Anticipation is high: it is the first night of Alternative Miss Ireland, being held as a fundraiser for the Rape Crisis Centre, which was set up in response to the gendered violence and homophobia widespread in Ireland in the 1980s.

Eurovision star Linda Martin stands on a stage in the shape of a long thin runway, in Sides nightclub on Dame Lane in the heart of Dublin's city centre. She checks her microphone, ensuring it's in perfect working order. A spirited crowd of giddy gays, lesbians and intrigued onlookers streams into the club, eagerly grabbing their drinks as they anticipate what promises to be an evening of sheer spectacle. Elsewhere in the venue, perched high above on scaffolding, Irish celebrity Twink, renowned fashion designer John Rocha, drag icon Mr Pussy and artist Kevin Sharkey sort out their judges' scoring system. Backstage (if one could call it that), numerous contestants are huddled together at the foot of a spiral staircase, confined within a space barely more than one hundred square feet.[6] The only thing separating them from the crowd slowly filling the venue is a thin curtain, behind which are nine nervous contestants, carefully but somewhat frantically moving around, fearful that their ensembles for the evening might rip or tear.[7]

Tonie Walsh is busy putting the finishing touches to his vision – Miss Demeanour Rathmines – and the hat he will wear in the daywear category, a replica of Rathmines Town Hall. Meanwhile, contestant Kitty Kelly has put together her 'scatty housewife' ensemble, ready to shock the audience.[8] The outrageous and fabulously curated looks venerated over the course of the night culminate in the crowning of Miss Isle as the very first winner of the AMI contest. Miss Isle, adorned with three missiles brimming with four gallons of fluorescent paint and flour, ready to create an explosive spectacle on stage, secured victory and a pair of tickets to New York. In doing so, she cemented her position as the inaugural champion of what would evolve into a cherished queer Irish cultural tradition.

After a hiatus of nine years AMI returned in 1996, reconstituted as an AIDS fundraiser and HIV consciousness-raising spectacle. Discussions around the re-emergence of AMI occurred towards the end of 1995, with a potential 1996 launch date being put on the table. Rory O'Neill was emerging onto the Irish drag scene as Panti Bliss and, alongside Niall Sweeney, had started contributing to an alternative club scene with their 'faux-fetish' club night, GAG.[9] GAG was produced by Rory, Niall, Tonie Walsh, Claire Crosbie and Karim White. (Claire Crosbie would become particularly important in the development of AMI, hosting AMI production weekends away. These consisted of 'think-ins', where the creatives involved in AMI came together to discuss ideas for each year, from themes to what was pragmatic in terms of budgets.)[10] Jason O'Connors of the Dublin AIDS Alliance had approached Panti, Niall and Trish Brennan to see if they would revitalise the competition, with the aim of using it as a fundraiser. Jason had been working with Tonie Walsh in *GCN* and initiated the conversation through the connections he made there.[11] The fact that this was for an AIDS charity was particularly important – some of the original contestants in the first AMI had died from AIDS-related complications. In March 1996 the Temple Bar Music Centre hosted the second AMI contest and started what would become an annual tradition, where AMI would take place on the Sunday before St Patrick's Day. That year's contest would establish a tradition for imaginative and boundary-breaking contestants – Miss Interpreted drove a motorbike into the venue through the loading-bay doors.

After its fantastic return, AMI III launched the next year at the Red Box venue in a former railway station on Harcourt Street. One of the standout contestants that year was Miss Shirley Temple Bar, who had decided to enter the competition at the encouragement of Panti. Shirley embarked on an imaginative journey to infuse humour into her performance. She developed a character portraying a twelve-year-old aspiring gymnast deeply committed to an anti-drugs stance due to her upbringing in Dublin's inner city. Her ultimate dream was to meet Twink. In her act, Shirley embarked on a quest that began with competing in the local community games and culminated with her eyes set on the Olympics.

In keeping with the community games concept, Shirley's swimwear saw her sporting verruca socks. The introduction of comedy into the performance brought the house down at Red Box. Her act was a mesmerising blend of skill, elegance and sheer hilarity. Adding to the humour, Brendan Courtney joined the performance, playfully carrying Shirley's Olympic medals – which were in fact Shirley's genuine community games medals from her childhood. Following her victory, Shirley secured a regular slot at The George, where her profile began to rise. Her bingo performances at the venue became extremely popular, eventually propelling her into the role of presenter on RTÉ's *Telly Bingo* in 2001.

Shirley's groundbreaking performance, marked by her unique brand of comedy, inspired future contestants. Katherine Lynch, a prospective AMI entrant, found herself accidentally and fabulously falling into the next year's competition, in 1998. Katherine had started an acting course and was working in the Smalltalk café when her fellow workers and manager Shane Harte said she would be a perfect contestant. 'But I'm not a gay man, I'm not a drag queen,' Katherine protested. 'You're camp, that's all you need.'[12] And so Katherine, Shane and her 'team' set to work on a £50 budget to buy every bit of red and white material in the city, and spent a number of night sewing Katherine's three looks, in what she refers to as a Laura Ashley/Dolly Parton factory. Out of that factory came Tampy Lilette, 'a periodically obsessed country-and-western star'.[13] Tampy Lilette, with her glamorous sense of irony and self-parody, was inspired by country music stars Tammy Wynette and Dolly Parton, with each performance from daywear to evening wear riffing off country classics. Tampy's final number encompassed a huge red dress with a big cut-out boat at the front, called *Ti-Tampion* and modelled on the *Titanic,* as she sang Bette Midler's 'Wind Beneath My Wings'. Against her own expectations, Katherine won, becoming the second woman to take the AMI Medusa crown, following AMI II's Miss Tress, bestowed on her by Shirley. In a kitsch display of rage, Miss Veda Beaux Reves, who had come runner-up, flung her bouquet at the judges' table, providing that year's competition with an unadulterated camp climax.[14] Veda would return the following year and emerge victorious at AMI V. Katherine looks back at AMI fondly: 'AMI was a community and family and we lived for it – that night lasted a week because we didn't go home. Only for that competition, I would never have gotten to where I am today. I owe my career to the gang there.'[15] Katherine's victory in AMI led to a cabaret-show residency at Gubu (the location where Pantibar is now situated), eventually launching her highly successful and enduring television career.

AMI played a pivotal role not only in launching long-term careers but also in fostering a diverse and inclusive community. The Filipino community in Ireland, which had seen rapid growth in the early 2000s due to targeted recruitment by the Irish health service, found a welcoming and inclusive space within the competition. This became evident when an Alternative Miss Philippines competition was introduced in 2002, serving as a feeder event for AMI and held each year at the theatre in Liberty Hall. The winner of the Alternative Miss Philippines competition earned the opportunity to compete in the AMI final, further highlighting the diverse and multicultural nature of the event.[16] The enclave of acceptance, fun and imagination within AMI and its queer community attracted prospective contestant Sinéad Burke in 2012. Sinéad, who has achondroplasia and faced discrimination due to how people treated her as a 'little person', had a transformative experience when she attended the Space'N'Veda show at The George.[17] Dancing on stage to Britney's 'Slave 4 U', Sinéad recalls being shocked because, 'Nothing happened. No one looked at me strangely. I wasn't pointed out. I was merely left alone to enjoy myself.'[18] This new-found sense of acceptance led to Sinéad entering an application for AMI the very next morning. She created her alter ego Minnie Mélange and set about retelling and subverting the story of *Snow White and the Seven Dwarfs* from her perspective, with seven dwarves who were all of average height. With a performance good to go, Minnie's début on the Olympia stage was introduced through a voice-over narration, announcing, 'Once upon a time, in a land far away, lived a little girl, who wasn't actually gay, But why did she enter? I hear you all say. Is she alternative? Why yes, she was born this way.'[19] Minnie's triumphant journey speaks to the transformative power of AMI as a platform for inclusion. Her description of AMI as an opportunity to engage with the accepting queer community underscores the profound impact of this community and cultural space. It highlights the potential of inclusive platforms like AMI to not only provide visibility and acceptance but also to challenge conventional norms and pave the way for a more diverse and open-minded society.

As the competition expanded, so did the venues. The Red Box nightclub setting proved to be challenging as the competition continued to grow, with contestants sometimes having to prepare in a tent in the nightclub's car park, enduring freezing conditions while waiting to go on stage.[20] By the turn of the millennium, AMI found its home in the Olympia Theatre, which enabled the production team to put the performances front and centre and let the contestants run wild. Almost like its straight brother, the GAA, AMI started to develop a local grassroots base, with regional heats. Competitions like Alternative Miss Cork, Alternative Miss Galway and Alternative Miss Limerick gave rise to a new generation of local queer talent across Ireland. The winners of these regional heats earned guaranteed spots in AMI, while money was raised at a local level for HIV charities. AMI also saw itself as an all-island event and made sure to have representation from Northern Ireland in the contest each year.

As a platform for emerging queer performers and a haven of inclusivity, AMI was undeniably transformative. However, the glamour and vibrancy of the show concealed the extensive behind-the-scenes efforts required to make it all happen, especially as AMI got bigger each year. This crucial work was well understood by the show's producer, Noel Sutton. Noel had attended the very first

AMI as a spectator and was mesmerised by the spectacle. Having been encouraged by Panti and Niall to enter AMI V as Miss Me_Tamorphosis in 1999, Noel found himself becoming more and more involved with production, and by 2002, he had taken over as producer. 'We never knew what was going to happen on that stage,' Noel says.[21] The role of producer was all-consuming, and from Christmas to March of each year, it became a full-time job. In addition, the creative process was year-round, and the AMI family had some of the most crazy, outlandish and phenomenally creative minds. Noel's challenge was to try and make as much of it happen within the confines of the little money they had for production. His first year was a trial by fire – literally. On the night of the competition, contestant Miss Monique incorporated fire-eating into her performance without telling production. Noel's health and safety concerns quickly rushed to the surface as he got the production team and volunteers to scramble backstage and search for buckets of sand in case fire engulfed the Olympia stage.[22] Another contestant appeared with a large live snake as part of her performance: Noel feared the creature would get loose and slither around the theatre, either backstage or rippling amongst the audience.

At the core of AMI was a conscience and heart. While the competition provided entertainment and enjoyment, it also served as a vital fundraising mechanism for AIDS and HIV charities. Many members of the AMI production team and the broader community had friends who were living with HIV and witnessed the challenges they faced. Furthermore, AMI aimed to be a commemoration of those lives lost to AIDS. Beyond the glamour and festivity, there was a profound commitment to raising funds. Ticket proceeds were channelled directly to charities, while the production side involved extensive fundraising efforts, from seeking sponsors to calling in favours from friends of AMI, all with the common goal of generating as much financial support as possible for organisations like the Dublin AIDS Alliance, Open Heart House, Cairde and the GUIDE Clinic at St James's hospital, Ireland's first STI clinic, with its adjoining Hospital 5 for a time being the ground zero of the Irish AIDS epidemic.

On Sunday, 18 March 2012, as Minnie Mélange celebrated her win, the final curtain descended on the Olympia stage, marking the end of AMI's remarkable journey – she had finally come of age. As the music came to a stop and the last resonating echoes of high-heeled footsteps gradually faded away, the Olympia stage stood empty. The chaotic beauty of AMI concluded on its silver jubilee, leaving in its wake cherished memories and a legacy that would be fondly remembered by all those who had the privilege of being part of this unique celebration of queer culture and creativity. AMI, like a shimmering looking glass, beautifully reflected the essence of this fabulous community, showcasing its resilience, creativity and indomitable spirit. In the spotlight of the AMI stage, the heart of Ireland's queer culture pulsated, radiating an unapologetic celebration of diversity and unity. It also proved that great change did not always have to be legislative and political. AMI ignited a spark that would transcend its dazzling performances and reverberate into the very fabric of societal transformation. It whispered a resounding truth: that the unbridled expression of joy could be an agent of change, inspiring a culture that embraced diversity, acceptance and the undiluted pursuit of happiness.

Alternative Miss Ireland Winners

Year	Number	Winner
1987	I	Miss Isle
1996	II	Miss Tress
1997	III	Miss Shirley Temple Bar
1998	IV	Miss Tampy Lilette
1999	V	Miss Veda Beaux Reves
2000	VI	Miss Siobhán Broadway
2001	VII	Miss Tina Leggs Tantrum
2002	VIII	Miss Sid Viscous
2003	IX	Miss Alter Ego
2004	X	Miss Twirly Chassy
2005	XI	Miss Heidi Konnt
2006	XII	Miss Funtime Gustavo
2007	XIII	Miss Joanna Ryde
2008	XIV	Miss Sheila Fits-Patrick
2009	XV	Miss Smilin' Kanker
2010	XVI	Miss Peaches Queen
2011	XVII	Miss Mangina Jones
2012	XVIII	Miss Minnie Mélange

Afterword

As I finished writing this book and was checking quotations with many of the people who gracefully told me their stories, one interviewee, Derek Byrne, wrote an email to me, saying: 'it is actually quite wonderful to have this story told in public for the first time in almost forty years and gives me a sense of closure on something which has always been at the back of my mind. For that, I am eternally grateful.' Derek's comment highlights how telling these stories of the LGBTQ community is not only empowering (and sometimes painful) but can contribute to a collective understanding of LGBTQ history and identity. As Ethan Mordden notes in the introduction to his short-story collection *Buddies*, 'all of gay life is stories'. This sentiment is very much at the heart of *Reeling in the Queers*. Stories that exist within the LGBTQ community, especially during a time when many queer people had to evade detection in a more oppressive society, risk erasure. It is crucial that these stories are recorded, written down, told again and then retold. Many of these stories remain hidden. Many have yet to be discovered. The stories included here are not 'absolute' histories of queer Ireland, but the events and people within them do provide a mirror and window: a mirror to broader Irish society and a window into a changing world, particularly for LGBTQ minorities.

What has emerged in this book is a small patchwork of stories, memories and recollections that connects to a broader and emerging tapestry of queer Irish history. In the last number of years, there has been a dedicated and sustained effort around recording, establishing and critically engaging with this history. This book dovetails with much of this work pertaining to LGBTQ life and culture in Ireland, and to this end, I would like to supply a guide to further reading.

Patrick McDonagh's *Gay and Lesbian Activism in the Republic of Ireland, 1973–93* delves into the activism of LGBTQ individuals involved in the political movement, underscoring how LGBTQ activists played a significant role in changing both legal and social aspects of Irish society during this period. Similarly, Abigail Fletcher's 'From Partition to Decriminalisation: Homosexuality in Northern Ireland' and Tom Hulme's 'Out of the Shadows: One Hundred Years of LGBT Life in Northern Ireland' provide significant insights into queer history in Northern Ireland, while Marian Duggan's *Queering Conflict: Examining Lesbian and Gay Experiences of Homophobia in Northern Ireland* examines how homophobia has emerged and been sustained during the latter half of the twentieth century.

More local, focused research has emerged through Orla Egan's *Queer Republic of Cork*, which accounts for the country's significant contribution to queer life in Ireland. Brian Lacey's *Terrible Queer Creatures: Homosexuality in Irish History* presents a long overview of queer Irish history, from pre-modern times until the early twenty-first century. Kieran Rose's *Diverse Communities: The Evolution of Lesbian and Gay Politics in Ireland* traces the development of LGBT organisations in Ireland until decriminalisation in 1993, while Íde O'Carroll and Eoin Collins's *Lesbian and Gay Visions of Ireland: Towards the Twenty-First Century* provides reflections on LGBT cultural and political life in Ireland at the end of the twentieth century.

Una Mullally's *In the Name of Love – The Movement for Marriage Equality in Ireland: An Oral History* and Sonja Tiernan's *The History of Marriage Equality in Ireland: A Social Revolution Begins* trace the more recent movement leading to the same-sex marriage referendum in 2015. Mary McAuliffe has examined the queer sexualities of women during the revolutionary period through her book *The Diaries of Kathleen Lynn: A Life Revealed through Personal Writing*. Averill Earls's forthcoming book *Love in the Lav: A Social Biography of Same-Sex Desire in Postcolonial Ireland* also accounts for a history of same-sex desire from the foundation of the State until the birth of a gay and lesbian civil rights movement.

Acknowledgements

I began writing this book at an important moment for queer Ireland: 2024 marks half a century since a formalised movement around gay and lesbian civil rights came together, setting in motion decades of activism, joy and fun, creating an enclave for those who came after, especially for young(ish) gay people like me. Much of this work, activism and dedication was unglamorous and hard, but as the last fifty years have demonstrated, a lot can change. While not perfect, Ireland has certainly become another country since 1974 for the LGBTQ community, so my thanks must firstly go to all who strove towards creating equality and spaces for many generations of LGBTQ people to find joy and community.

Reeling in the Queers started as a seed of an idea that could grow into something tangible and decent if someone was willing to give it a chance. I am beyond thrilled that Aoife K. Walsh of New Island Books saw the potential in the slush pile and gave *Reeling in the Queers* a home. I will be eternally thankful to her for providing a space for these stories to be heard and for seeing a value in queer history for a mainstream press. Too often projects like this get side-lined or overlooked. Thank you to New Island for going against the grain. Significant, countless, abundant thanks to Djinn von Noorden for the meticulous and careful editing and making the process of rewrites not as painstaking as it tends to be. To Mariel Deegan, Des Doyle and Cassia Gaden Gilmartin for steering this book into the 'real world'.

Many seasoned activists, historians, archivists and members of Ireland's LGBTQ community have supported this project along the way and I am beyond grateful to work alongside a group of very encouraging, collaborative individuals who are as passionate about queer Irish culture as I am. Sara Philips of the Irish Trans Archive has helped this project in more ways than one, from helping to shape a number of chapters and perspectives, all the way down to providing fact-checking and clarification. Orla Egan of the Cork LGBT Archive also provided guidance. Cathal Kerrigan, Karl Hayden and Rita Wild have kindly spent a number of hours on the phone with me, working out intellectual knots and sequencing events into broader queer Irish history. Patrick McDonagh was similarly as helpful and supportive as he always has been since we were both young PhD scholars foraging our way through this rich history. I particularly thank him for some last-minute amendments and additions to the Irish queer history timeline. Tonie Walsh has been an especially steadfast supporter of this project from day one, being one of the first to hear what was then a half-baked idea. He has consistently offered valuable consultancy, unwavering support, essential archival materials and, most importantly, his enduring friendship, extending his contributions from his time in both Dublin and Antalya, Turkey.

I am very grateful to those who agreed to be interviewed for this research and who gave over an enormous amount of time, trusting me with their stories over some tears and mostly laughter. Sadly, some are now deceased. In light of this, I would like to pay particular respects to Terri Blanche, who is mentioned at several points throughout this book. Terri was crucial to early gay and lesbian activism, often as a lone lesbian voice in a movement dominated by men. From my interviews with people throughout the community, Terri's creation of space and being a shining 'lesbian' light was crucial for bringing so many women into the fold. How lucky I was to speak with her before she passed and hear her story. May we remember all that she did. Similarly, Edmund Lynch, one of the founders of the IGRM is no longer with us. I do miss his calls and our coffees in the Irish Film Institute and the West End Café, Temple Bar.

I would not have written *Reeling in the Queers* were it not for the support given to me by the School of Information and Communication Studies at UCD, a school to which I proudly belong. In particular, I must thank dear colleagues and friends: Claire McGuinness who read each chapter and provided feedback at every step and Marguerite Barry for reading an early draft proposal. Thanks also to Amber Cushing, Eugenia Siapera,

Crystal Fulton, Elizabeth Farries, Faye Carrie, Stefanie Havelka, Kalpana Shankar, Marco Bastos, Benjamin Cowan, Lai Ma, Susan Leavy, Judith Wusteman, James Steinhoff, Pat Brodie, Kevin Doherty, Odile Dumbleton, Brendan Spillane, Arjumund Yonus, Claire Nolan, Lisa Gaffney and Fiona Smyth. Thanks to my PhD students, who have taught me so much: Christo Thomas Jacob, Romeo Fraccari, Aoife Quinn Hegarty, Hanxiao Zhang and Yifei Yang.

To my friends and our friendships, in all their fun and vibrant manifestations: Michael Cleary-Gaffney, Dean Phelan, Denis Vaughan, Jennifer Boyle, Megan O'Shea, Michelle Hendy, Aisling Boland, Kim Fitzgerald, Brenda O'Connell, Maria Pramaggiore, Rachael Kelly, Rodrigo Nascimento, Denis O'Driscoll, Laura Byrne, Lauren O'Donovan, Áine McManus, Alan Cawley, Peter Lynch, Siobhán Buckley, Áine McAdam, Emma Fenton, Anderson Alves de Silva, Stephen O'Neill, Bill Hughes, Pranjal Singh, Ciara Buckle, Kristal McNamara and Simon Orrock.

To my family: my brothers, John and Nigel, in-laws Dave and Orlaith, and my parents, Pat and Helena, who have always been a source of encouragement and support. And to my Cork family: Maria, John, Dermot, Orla and Kieran Lynch.

And finally, for Baxter and Barry: Baxter, a faithful (albeit sleepy) writing companion and perfect listener (possibly reluctant?) to my 'thinking-out-loud' on chapter drafts. And Barry, my husband, this book's first reader, for more than I will ever be able to write here on this page.

Select Bibliography

Archives
Cork LGBT Archive
David Norris Personal Papers, National Library of Ireland
Edmund Lynch's LGBTQ Oral History Archive
Gay Community News Archive
Irish Trans Archive
Irish Queer Archive, National Library of Ireland
LGBT History Northern Ireland Archive

Personal Papers
Claire Hackett Personal Archive
Cathal Kerrigan Personal Archive
Kieran Rose Personal Archive
Tonie Walsh Personal Archive

Newspapers/Periodicals
Belfast Telegraph
Daily Mirror
Evening Herald
Gay Community News
Gay Ireland
Gralton
Munster GCN
Notches
OUT
Pride 1996: The Official Publication of the 1993 London Pride March and Festival
Southern Star
Sunday Independent

Sunday World
The Evening Press
The Female Impersonator
The Guardian
The Irish Examiner
The Irish Independent
The Irish Press
The Irish Times
The Journal.ie
The Nationalist and Leinster Times
The New York Times
The Pink Paper
The Vacuum

Visual Sources
Access Community Television (RTÉ).
A Different Country, dir. Edmund Lynch (RTÉ: It's a Wrap Productions, 2017).
Eurotrash (Channel 4).
Rock Hudson: All That Heaven Allowed, dir. Stephen Kijack (HBO: Altitude Film Entertainment, 2023).
The Late Late Show (RTÉ).
The Love That Dare Not Speak Its Name, dir. Bill Hughes (RTÉ: Radius Television, 2000).

Oral History Interviews
Terri Blanche
Tom Brace
Toni Burgess
Derek Byrne
John Calnan
Maurice Clarke
Davina Devine
Heather Fleming
Bill Foley
Claire Hackett
Louise Hannon
Mary Kelly
William Kennedy
Cathal Kerrigan

Bernárd Lynch
Katherine Lynch
Phil Moore
Murf
David Norris
Pauline O'Donnell
Mark Power
Kieran Rose
Eamon Somers
Noel Sutton
Tonie Walsh
Rita Wild

Secondary Sources

Alternative Miss Ireland: Dancing at the Crossroads (Dublin: X Communications, 2004).

Armstrong, Elizabeth A. and Suzanna M. Crage. 'Movements and Memory: The Making of the Stonewall Myth'. *American Sociological Review*, 71.5 (2006), pp. 724–51.

Atherton Lin, Jeremy. *Gay Bar: Why We Went Out* (London: Granta, 2021).

Banotti, Mary. *There's Something About Mary* (Dublin: Currach Press, 2008).

Carter, David. *Stonewall: The Riots That Sparked the Gay Revolution* (New York: St Martin's Press, 2004).

Casey, Maurice J. 'Radical Politics and Gay Activism in the Republic of Ireland, 1974–1990'. *Irish Studies Review*, 26.2 (2018), pp. 217–36.

Castells, Manuel. *The City and the Grassroots: A Cross-Cultural Theory of Urban Social Movements* (Berkeley: University of California Press, 1983).

Crangle, Jack, Fearghus Roulston, Graham Dawson, Liam Harte and Barry Hazley. 'Somewhere Bigger and Brighter? Ambivalence and Desire in Memories of Leaving the North of Ireland during the Troubles'. *Irish Studies Review*, 30.3 (2022), pp. 259–79.

Cronin, Michael G. *Sexual/Liberation*. (Cork: Cork University Press, 2022).

Cushing, Amber L. and Páraic Kerrigan. 'Extending the PIM-B Concept: An Exploration of How Nonbinary People Maintain Personal Information Over Time'. In Isaac Sserwanga et al. (eds),

Information for a Better World: Normality, Virtuality, Physicality, Inclusivity. iConference 2023. Lecture Notes in Computer Science, 13971 (Cham: Springer, 2023).

Dublin Lesbian and Gay Men's Collective. *Out for Ourselves: The Lives of Irish Lesbians & Gay Men* (Dublin: Women's Community Press, 1986).

Duggan, Marian. *Queering Conflict: Examining Lesbian and Gay Experiences of Homophobia in Northern Ireland* (Surrey and Burlington: Ashgate Publishing, 2012).

Earls, Averill. *Love in the Lav: A Social Biography of Same-Sex Desire in Postcolonial Ireland* (Philadelphia: Temple University Press, forthcoming).

Egan, Orla. *Queer Republic of Cork: Cork's Lesbian, Gay, Bisexual and Transgender Communities, 1970s–1990s* (Cloghroe: Onstream, 2016).

Ekins, Richard and King, Dave, 'Virginia Prince: Transgender Pioneer', *International Journal of Transgenderism*, 8.4 (2005), pp. 5-15

Fahie, Declan. '"Spectacularly Exposed and Vulnerable" – How Irish Equality Legislators Subverted the Personal and Professional Security of Lesbian, Gay and Bisexual Teachers'. *Sexualities*, 19.4 (2016), pp. 393–411.

Farrell, Michael. 'Lydia Foy and the Struggle for Gender Recognition: A Case Study in Public Interest Litigation'. *Socio-Legal Studies Review*, 1 (2015), pp. 153–9.

Ferriter, Diarmaid. *Occasions of Sin: Sex and Society in Modern Ireland* (London: Profile Books, 2009).

Fletcher, Abigail. *From Partition to Decriminalisation: Homosexuality in Northern Ireland*. Ph.D. Thesis, University of Edinburgh. Unpublished.

Górnicka, Barbara and Mark Doyle. *Sex and Sexualities in Ireland: Interdisciplinary Perspectives* (Oxon: Palgrave, 2023).

Hanscombe, Gillian. 'The Right to Lesbian Parenthood'. *Journal of Medical Ethics*, 9 (1983), pp. 133–5.

Harsin Drager, Emmett and Lucas Platero. 'At the Margins of Time and Place: Transsexuals and the Transvestites in Trans Studies'. *Transgender Studies Quarterly*, 8.4 (2021), pp. 417–25.

Hertzog, Mark. *The Lavender Vote: Lesbians, Gay Men and Bisexuals in American Electoral Politics* (New York: NYU Press, 1996).

Hulme, Tom. 'Queering Family History and the Lives of Irish Men Before Gay Liberation'. *The History of the Family*, DOI: 10.1080/1081602X.2023.2297699 (2024).

Hulme, Tom. 'Out of the Shadows: One Hundred Years of LGBT Life in Northern Ireland' (In *Northern Ireland 1921–2021: Centenary Historical Perspectives* Belfast: Ulster Historical Foundation, 2022).

Kelly, Brendan. 'Homosexuality and Irish Psychiatry: Medicine, Law and the Changing Face of Ireland'. *Irish Journal of Psychological Medicine*, 34.3 (2017), pp. 209–15.

Lacey, Brian. *Terrible Queer Creatures: Homosexuality in Irish History* (Dublin: Wordwell, 2015).

Lapovsky Kennedy, Elizabeth and Madeline D. Davis. *Boots of Leather, Slippers of Gold: The History of a Lesbian Community, 20th Anniversary Edition* (London and New York: Routledge, 2014).

Lauria, Mickey and Lawrence Knopp. 'Toward an Analysis of the Role of Gay Communities in the Urban Renaissance'. *Urban Geography*, 6.2 (1985), pp. 152–69.

Leane, Máire and Elizabeth Kiely. *Sexualities and Irish Society: A Reader* (Dublin: Orpen Press, 2014).

Lynch, Father Bernárd. *A Priest on Trial* (London: Bloomsbury, 1993).

Macleod, Allison. *Irish Queer Cinema* (Edinburgh: Edinburgh University Press, 2018).

McAuliffe, Mary. *The Diaries of Kathleen Lynn: A Life Revealed Through Personal Writing* (Dublin: UCD Press, 2023).

McDonagh, Patrick. *Gay and Lesbian Activism in the Republic of Ireland, 1973–1993* (London: Bloomsbury, 2021).

McLaughlin, Noel and Martin McLoone. 'From Men to Boys: Masculinity, Politics and the Irish Boy Band'. In Conn Holohan and Tony Tracy (eds), *Masculinity and Irish Popular Culture: Tiger's Tales* (London: Palgrave, 2014).

Molloy, Karina with Kathryn Rogers. *A Woman in Defence* (Dublin: Hachette Books Ireland, 2023).

Mordden, Ethan. *Buddies* (New York: St. Martin's Griffin, 1982).

Mullally, Una. *In the Name of Love – The Movement for Marriage Equality in Ireland: An Oral History* (Dublin: The History Press, 2014).

Mullen, Patrick R. *The Poor Bugger's Tool: Irish Modernism, Queer Labour and Postcolonial History* (Oxford: Oxford University Press, 2012).

Newsome, W. Jake. *Pink Triangle Legacies: Coming Out in the Shadow of the Holocaust* (Ithaca and London: Cornell University Press, 2022).

Norris, David. *A Kick Against the Pricks: The Autobiography* (Dublin: Transworld Ireland, 2012).

O'Carroll, Íde and Eoin Collins. *Lesbian and Gay Visions of Ireland: Towards the Twenty-First Century* (London: Cassell, 1995).

Ó Drisceoil, Donal. '"The Best Banned in the Land": Censorship and Irish Writing Since 1950'. *The Yearbook of English Studies*, 35 (2005), pp. 146–60.

Philpott, Ger. *Deep End* (Dublin: Poolbeg Press, 1995).

Polikoff, Nancy. 'Lesbian Mothers, Lesbian Families: Legal Obstacles, Legal Challenges'. *New York University Review of Law & Social Change*, 14.4 (2021), pp. 907–14.

Robinson, Pádraig. *Gaze Against Imperialism* (Sacramento, California: Metaflux, 2019).

Rose, Kieran. *Diverse Communities: The Evolution of Lesbian and Gay Politics in Ireland* (Cork: Cork University Press, 1994).

Shilts, Randy. *The Mayor of Castro Street: The Life and Times of Harvey Milk* (London: Atlantic Books, 2022).

Storm, Judith. 'It's No Blarney: Irish TV Scene Lacking'. *Renaissance*, 9.10 (1995), p. 1-2.

The New York Public Library, *The Stonewall Reader*. (New York: Penguin, 2019).

Tiernan, Sonja. *The History of Marriage Equality in Ireland: A Social Revolution Begins* (Manchester: University of Manchester Press, 2020).

Toops, Jessica. '"Living Lives of Quiet Desperation": Accounts of Gay Men and Lesbians during the Troubles'. *Western Illinois Historical Review*, 6 (Spring 2014), pp. 37-82.

Villar-Argáiz, Pilar. *Irishness on the Margins: Minority and Dissident Identities* (Oxon: Palgrave, 2018).

Walsh, Fintan. *Queer Performance and Contemporary Ireland: Dissent and Disorientation* (London and New York: Palgrave, 2016).

Walshe, Éibhear. *Sex, Nation and Dissent in Irish Writing* (New York: St. Martin's Press, 1997).

Notes

Introduction

1. Aleksandra Eriksson, 'So What if the Irish PM Is Gay?', *EU Observer*, 14 June 2017, https://euobserver.com/lgbti/138132; Pilar Villar-Argáiz, *Irishness on the Margins: Minority and Dissident Identities* (Oxon: Palgrave, 2018).

2. Oral history interview with Claire Hackett.

1. 'The Two Mothers Got Together and Sorted It Out': Phil Moore, Parents Enquiry and Gay Law Reform

1. *The Late Late Show*, 1989 (RTÉ, 1 December).

2. Ibid.

3. Ibid.

4. Oral history interview with Phil Moore.

5. Phil Moore, 'Parents', in Dublin Lesbian and Gay Men's Collectives, *Out for Ourselves: The Lives of Irish Lesbians & Gay Men* (Dublin: Women's Community Press, 1986), p. 135.

6. Ibid.

7. *Access Community Television*, RTÉ Archive Reference 96D00716 (RTÉ, 16 February 1984).

8. Oral history interview with Phil Moore.

9. David Norris Personal Papers, National Library of Ireland, Acc. 6672 Box 36: 'Working Paper on Gay Youth Group by Bernard Keogh, September 1979'.

10. Oral history interview with Phil Moore.

11. Peter Tatchell, 'Rose Robertson: An Obituary', *The Guardian*, 26 October 2011.

12. Kathleen O'Meara, 'Parents Have Nothing to Do with It', *The Irish Times*, 31 August 1984.

13. Oral history interview with Phil Moore.

14. Ibid.

15. Ibid.

16. Ibid.

17. During the gay law reform years of 1988–93, the age of consent for sex between gay men was a politically contested issue. GLEN and other Irish gay civil rights groups campaigned for an age of consent that would reflect the law for heterosexual people, which was 17. Many members of the government at the time wanted the higher age of consent of 21.

18. Oral history interview with Phil Moore.

19. Mary Banotti, *There's Something About Mary* (Dublin: Currach Press, 2008), p. 45.

20. Oral history interview with Phil Moore.

21. Ibid.

22. Ibid.

2. Out of the Closet and into a Boy Band: 4Guyz and the Pursuit of 1990s Pop Stardom

1. 'Boyz to Play GAY', *Gay Community News*, issue 72, April 1995.

2. Ibid.

3. '4Guyz – Biographies'. Junior Larkin qtd on Matt & Andrej Koymasky Home – The Living Room. Available at: http://andrejkoymasky.com/liv/fam/biof2/four01.html

4. Dermot Hayes, *Evening Herald*, 10 January 1996.

5. Richie Taylor, 'Gayzone', *Daily Mirror*, 8 February 1996.

6. Derek Keegan, '4Guyz on the Rise', *Gay Community News*, issue 83, April 1996, p. 5.

7. Oral history interview with Mark Power, July 2023.

8. Noel McLaughlin and Martin McLoone, 'From Men to Boys: Masculinity, Politics and the Irish Boy Band', in Conn Holohan and Tony Tracy (eds), *Masculinity and Irish Popular Culture: Tiger's Tales* (London: Palgrave, 2014).

9. Richie Taylor, 'Now It's Gayzone; Protest Band 4Guyz Set to Face the World', *Daily Mirror*, 22 March 1996.

10. Aileen O'Reilly, 'Five Guys Come Out of the Closet', *Evening Herald*, 2 March 1996.

11. Oral history interview with Mark Power.

12. Ibid.

13. Ibid.

14. Oral history interview with Mark Power.

15. 'Gay Band Get Rose Week Ban', *Sunday Independent*, 2 June 1996.

16. Aileen O'Reilly, 'No Tralee Joy for 4Guyz', *Evening Herald*, 4 June 1996.

17. Ibid.

18. Oral history interview with Mark Power.

19. Aileen O'Reilly, 'Guyz Lashed, by George!', *Evening Herald*, 12 July 1996.

20. David Pollard, 'Queer Year', *Pride 1996: The Official Publication of the 1993 London Pride March and Festival*, June 1996.

21. Claire Grady, '4Guyz Audition for the Perfect Number 5: It Could Be You', *Evening Herald*, 25 June 1996.

22. Aileen O'Reilly, 'And Then There Were Five Again … Almost', *Evening Herald*, 28 June 1996.

23. Aileen O'Reilly, '4Guyz Hit the Bee Gee Trail', *Evening Herald*, 18 September 1996.

24. Derek Keegan, 'Exit 4Guyz, Enter Pisces', *Gay Community News*, issue 92, February 1997, p. 3.

25. Barry Egan, 'Still Zrazy after All These Years', *Irish Independent*, 17 January 2016.

26. Ibid.

3. 'Bent Politicians': Gay and Lesbian Candidates in 1980s Electoral Politics

1. Oral history interview with Tonie Walsh.

2. Mark Hertzog, *The Lavender Vote: Lesbians, Gay Men and Bisexuals in American Electoral Politics* (New York: NYU Press, 1996).

3. David Norris, *A Kick Against the Pricks: The Autobiography* (Dublin: Transworld Ireland, 2012), p. 228.

4. Randy Shilts, *The Mayor of Castro Street: The Life and Times of Harvey Milk* (London: Atlantic Books, 2022).

5. Lillian Faderman, *Harvey Milk: His Lives and Death* (New Haven and London: Yale University Press, 2018).

6. Norris, p. 229.

7. Norris, p. 231.

8. Patrick McDonagh, *Gay and Lesbian Activism in the Republic of Ireland, 1973–1993* (London: Bloomsbury, 2021).

9. Ibid.

10. Mary Maher, 'They Are All Women's Issues in the End', *The Irish Times*, 12 June 1981.

11. Frank McDonald, 'Someone's Got to Go in Garret's Area', *The Irish Times*, 10 June 1981.

12. Interview with Tonie Walsh, 27 January 2022.

13. Irish Queer Archive, National Library of Ireland, MS 45, 976/3, GLEN Manifesto, 1989, General Election.

14. 'Gay Candidates in Irish Elections', *The Pink Paper*, 10 June 1989.

15. Elections Ireland, 26th Dáil 1989. Available at: https://electionsireland. org/result.cfm?election=1989&cons=104

16. Lisa Connell, 'Out, Proud & Independent' from the 2009 Local Election – South West Inner City. *Irish Election Literature*. Available at: https:// irishelectionliterature.com/2010/07/07/lisa-connell-out-proud-independ- ent-from-the-2009-le-south-west-inner-city/

17. Liam Clarke, 'Three Gay Politicians on Newly Elected Belfast City Council', *Belfast Telegraph*, 26 May 2014.

4. 'The Dowager Queen of the Transvestites': Judith Storm and Gender Diversity in Late-Twentieth-Century Ireland

1. Anthony McGrath, 'Any Man in the Storm'? *Gay Community News*, issue 64, July 1994, p. 10.

2. Ibid.

3. 'Feature: Interview with Judith Storm', *Gay Community News*, issue 18, May 1990, p. 9.

4. Transgender Equality Network of Ireland (TENI), 'Transvestite & Crossdressing'. Available at: https://teni.ie/resources/transvestite-and- crossdressing/.

5. Cristan Williams, 'Transgender', *Transgender Studies Quarterly*, 1.1–2 (2014), pp. 232–4.

6. Emmett Harsin Drager and Lucas Platero, 'At the Margins of Time and Place: Transsexuals and the Transvestites in Trans Studies', *Transgender Studies Quarterly*, 8.4 (2021), p. 417

7. Ibid.

8. McGrath, p. 10.

9. Richard Ekins and Dave King, 'Virginia Prince: Transgender Pioneer', *International Journal of Transgenderism*, 8.4 (2005), pp. 5–15.

10. Judith Storm, 'The Word from Dear Old Ireland', *The Female Impersonator,* no. 22, 1978.

11. Ibid.

12. Ibid.

13. Ibid

14. Ibid.

15. Ibid.

16. 'Storm over Transvestite on RTÉ's *Late Late*', *Irish Independent*, 12 February 1979.

17. 'That's No Lady, That's My Husband': 'The Highly Secret World of Ireland Transvestites', *Sunday World*, 20 November 1983.

18. Mairead Carey, 'The TVs are the only ones wearing skirts', *The Irish Press*, 15 September 1992.

19. Sara R. Philips, 'This #TransgenderAwarenessWeek We Look Back at Ireland's First Trans Groups Friends of Eon', *Gay Community News*. Available at: https://gcn.ie/this-transgenderawarenessweek-we-look-back-at-irelands-first-trans-group-friends-of-eon.

20. While the Friends of Eon is one of the most significant trans organisations in Irish trans history, its story is expansive and complex and accordingly would require significant space beyond the size of one chapter such as this. It's referenced here to demonstrate the developing and growing trans movement that Judith Storm intersected with at varying points.

21. Judith Storm, 'To Dress or Not to Dress'. *Gay Community News*, issue 1, February 1988, p. 7.

22. Ibid.

23. Oral history interview with Mary Kelly.

24. Letter from Judith Storm of the National Transvestite Group to Gay Information Cork at Quay Co-Op, Irish Trans Archive, 20 July 1986.

25. Judith Storm, 'To Dress or Not to Dress'. *Gay Community News*, issue 1, February 1988, p. 7.

26. Ibid.

27. Judith Storm, 'Clean Out of My Wig', *Gay Community News*, issue 41, June 1992, p. 13.

28. Maurice Newman, 'Boys will be Girls', clipping of article available in the Irish Trans Archive.

29. McGrath, p. 10.

30. 'Feature: Interview with Judith Storm', *Gay Community News*, issue 18, May 1990, p. 9.

31. McGrath, p. 10.

32. Maurice Newman, 'Boys Will Be Girls', clipping of article available in the Irish Trans Archive.

33. Ibid.

34. McGrath, p. 10.

35. 'Feature: Interview with Judith Storm', *Gay Community News*, issue 18, May 1990, p. 9.

36. Noirín Hegarty, 'Men in Dresses', *Evening Herald*, 1 October 1994.

37. 'The George Door Policy', *Gay Community News*, issue 108, July 1998, p. 36;

38. Anthony McGrath, 'Any Man in the Storm'? *Gay Community News*, issue 64, July 1994, p. 10.

39. Judith Storm, 'It's No Blarney. Irish TV Scene Lacking', *Renaissance*, 9.10 (1995), p. 1.

40. Storm, 1992.

5. A Private Matter? Gay Soldiers in the Irish Army

1. PJ Brennan, 'Gay Privates on Parade', *Gay Community News*, issue 17, April 1990, p. 8.

2. Ibid.

3. David Norris, 'Nothing Wrong with It', *Irish Independent*, 28 January 1993.

4. *A Different Country*, dir. Edmund Lynch (RTÉ, 2017).

5. Oral history interview with Tom Brace.

6. *A Different Country*, dir. Edmund Lynch (RTÉ, 2017).

7. *A Different Country*, dir. Edmund Lynch (RTÉ, 2017).

8. Oral history interview with Tom Brace.

9. Karina Molloy, with Kathryn Rogers, *A Woman in Defence* (Dublin: Hachette Books Ireland, 2023).

10. Kitty Holland, 'Defence Forces Honour Women's Role', *The Irish Times*, 10 December 2010.

11. Christina Finn and Niall O'Connor, 'An Organisation That "Barely Tolerates" Women: Report Details Extent of Abuse in Defence Forces', *The Journal.ie*, 28 March 2023.

12. 'Should Gays Be in the Army?, *Irish Independent*, 28 January 1993.

13. Ibid.

14. 'A Private Matter', *Irish Independent*, 28 January 1993.

15. Ibid.

16. Jim Cusack, 'Review of Gays in Army Possible', *The Irish Times*, 29 January 1993.

17. Geraldine Kennedy, 'Defence Forces Not to Be Exempted in Lifting Gays Ban', *The Irish Times*, 4 June 1993.

18. Mary Kenny, 'Gays: They're Simply Not the Same', *Irish Independent*, 22 May 1993.

19. Denis Coghlan, *The Irish Times*, 23 June 1993.

20. Ray Managh and Charles Mallon, 'Gay Row Hits Army', *Evening Herald*, 2 December 1993; 'Judgment Reserved in Homosexual Soldier Case', *The Irish Times*, 6 December 1994.

21. Ray Managh and Charles Mallon, 'Gay Row Hits Army', *Evening Herald*, 2 December 1993.

22. *C. v Convening Authority*, [1998] Courts-Martial Appeal Court [No. 3 C.M. of 1994]. Available at: https://ie.vlex.com/vid/c-v-convening-authority-802974269

23. Suzy Byrne, 'Homophobia in Uniform?' *Gay Community News*, issue 57, November 1993, p. 3.

24. Oral history interview with William Kennedy.

25. Ibid.

26. Ibid.

27. Ibid.

28. Commission on the Defence Forces, Report of the Commission on the Defence Forces, 2022. Available at: https://www.military.ie/en/public-information/publications/report-of-the-commission-on-defence-forces/report-of-the-commission-on-defence-forces.pdf.

29. 'Defence Forces Want More Women, Gay People and Ethnic Minorities', *The Journal.ie*, 4 August 2015. Available at: https://www.thejournal.ie/defence-force-recruitment-2252815-Aug2015/.

30. Mark O'Regan, Defence Forces to Let Gay Staff wed on Military Bases', *The Irish Examiner*, 22 May 2016. Available at: https://www.

independent.ie/irish-news/defence-forces-to-let-gay-staff-wed-on-military-bases/34735903.html.

6. Pink Carnations and Pink Triangles: The Emergence of Pride in Ireland (1974–1982)

1. Oral history interview with John Calnan.
2. Amy Blaney, 'Dublin Pride: Tens of Thousands March through City to Celebrate LGBTQ+ Rights', *Irish Independent*. Available at: https://www.independent.ie/regionals/dublin/dublin-news/dublin-pride-tens-of-thousands-march-through-city-to-celebrate-lgbtq-rights/a1093066156.html.
3. The New York Public Library, *The Stonewall Reader*. (New York: Penguin, 2019).
4. David Carter, *Stonewall: The Riots That Sparked the Gay Revolution* (New York: St Martin's Press, 2004).
5. Elizabeth A. Armstrong and Suzanna M. Crage, 'Movements and Memory: The Making of the Stonewall Myth', *American Sociological Review*, 71.5 (2006), pp. 724–51.
6. Meg Metcalf, 'The History of Pride', Library of Congress. Available at: https://www.loc.gov/ghe/cascade/index.html?appid=90dcc35abb71 4a24914c68c9654adb67
7. Ibid.
8. Patrick McDonagh, *Gay and Lesbian Activism in the Republic of Ireland, 1973–1993* (London: Bloomsbury, 2021), p. 18.
9. Ibid.
10. Ibid.
11. Oral history interview with David Norris.
12. McDonagh, p. 55.
13. Irish Queer Archive, National Library of Ireland, MS 45, 955/2, National Gay Federation, Pride Week 1979.
14. Ibid.
15. Ibid.
16. Irish Queer Archive, National Library of Ireland National Gay Federation, Gay Rights: It's Time', information leaflet, Gay Pride Week 1980.
17. Oral history interview with Tonie Walsh.
18. Sarah Prager, 'Four Flowering Plants That Have Been Decidedly Queer', *Politics and History, JSTOR Daily*, 29 January 2020.

19. Irish Queer Archive, National Library of Ireland National Gay Federation 'Gay Rights: It's Time', information leaflet, Gay Pride Week 1980.

20. Ibid.

21. Oral history interview with Eamon Somers.

22. Oral history interview with Murf.

23. Irish Queer Archive, National Library of Ireland, MS 45, 955/2, National Gay Federation Pride Week 1979.

24. Oral history interview with Murf.

25. Irish Queer Archive, National Library of Ireland, MS 45, 964/3, 'Gay Pride Week Pub Zap', NGF Newsletter 4 (July 1982).

26. Oral history interview with Murf.

27. W. Jake Newsome, *Pink Triangle Legacies: Coming Out in the Shadow of the Holocaust* (Ithaca and London: Cornell University Press, 2022), p. 2.

28. Oral history interview with Tonie Walsh.

29. McDonagh, p. 73.

30. Oral history interview with Kieran Rose.

31. Ibid.

32. McDonagh, p. 73.

7. The AIDS Priest and His Ministry: The Story of Fr Bernárd Lynch

1. Oral history interview with Fr Bernárd Lynch.

2. *The Late Late Show*, 3 April 1987 (Dublin: RTÉ).

3. Oral history interview with Fr Bernárd Lynch.

4. Ibid.

5. Father Bernárd Lynch, *A Priest on Trial* (Bloomsbury: London, 1993)

6. Lawrence K. Altman, 'Rare Cancer Seen in 41 Homosexuals', *The New York Times*, 25 May 1983.

7. Centers for Disease Control & Prevention (CDC), *Morbidity and Mortality Weekly Report*, 30.25 (3 July 1981), pp. 305–8.

8. Oral history interview with Fr Bernárd Lynch.

9. *Cork Examiner*, 18 February 1985; *The Irish Times*, 5 February 1985; *Evening Herald*, 13 February 1985; *Evening Press*, 1 February 1985; *Evening Press*, 5 February 1985; *Irish Press*, 8 February 1985.

10. 'Hudson Has AIDS, Spokesman Says', *The New York Times*, 26 July 1985.

11. *The Nationalist and Leinster Times*, 26 June 1985.

12. Oral history interview with Fr Bernárd Lynch.

13. Lynch, p. 41.

14. *The Late Late Show*, 3 April 1987 (Dublin: RTÉ).

15. Ibid.

16. AIDS Diary, New York City 1986, personal archive of Fr Bernárd Lynch.

17. 'The AIDS Priest', *Evening Herald*, 30 November 1987.

18. Ibid.

19. Oral history interview with Fr Bernárd Lynch.

20. Ibid.

21. Lynch, p. 53.

22. Oral history interview with Fr Bernárd Lynch.

23. Cardinal Joseph Ratzinger, 'Letter to the Bishops of the Catholic Church on the Pastoral Care of Homosexual Persons', Congregation for the Doctrine of the Faith. Available at: https://www.vatican.va/roman_curia/congregations/cfaith/documents/rc_con_cfaith_doc_19861001_homosexual-persons_en.html.

24. Oral history interview with Fr Bernárd Lynch.

25. Ibid.

26. Ibid.

27. HIV/AIDS Timeline, New York City AIDS Memorial. Available at: https://www.nycaidsmemorial.org/timeline.

8. Close Encounters of a Hollywood Kind: Rock Hudson and the Early Irish Gay Scene

1. This narrativisation and Michael's account is based on an article that originally appeared in *Gay Ireland* magazine in November 2001, titled 'Rock Hudson's Irish Weekend'. *Gay Ireland* was founded and produced by Brian Finnegan in 2001. The original article has no by-line, so I am referencing *Gay Ireland* in general.

2. Richard Meyer, 'Rock Hudson's Body', in Diana Fuss (ed.), *Inside/Out: Lesbian Theories, Gay Theories* (Routledge: London and New York, 1991).

3. *Rock Hudson: All That Heaven Allowed*, dir. Stephen Kijack (HBO: Altitude Film Entertainment, 2023).

4. Sam McGrath, 'Pubs and Gay Social Life in Dublin (1923–1973)', *The Irish Pub: Invention and Re-Invention* (Cork: Cork University Press, forthcoming).

5. *The Love That Dare Not Speak Its Name*, Bill Hughes (dir.), Radius Television (RTÉ, 2000).

6. 'Rock Hudson's Irish Weekend', *Gay Ireland*, November 2001.

7. David Norris, *A Kick Against the Pricks: The Autobiography* (Dublin: Transworld Ireland, 2012), p. 79.

8. 'Rock Hudson's Irish Weekend', *Gay Ireland*, November 2001.

9. Ibid.

10. McGrath.

11. Ibid.

12. Paul Candon, 'Reeling in the Years', *Gay Community News*, issue 1, 1988, p. 20.

13. McGrath, p. 9.

14. McGrath, p. 13.

15. Quoted by Hugh Oram, *The Irish Times*, 12 March 2007.

16. Oral history interview with Maurice Clarke.

17. Oral history interview with Terri Blanche.

18. Oral history interview with Bill Foley.

19. Oral history interview with Maurice Clarke.

20. Jeremy Atherton Lin, *Gay Bar: Why We Went Out* (London: Granta, 2021), p. 38.

21. Elizabeth Lapovsky Kennedy and Madeline D. Davis, *Boots of Leather, Slippers of Gold: The History of a Lesbian Community, 20th Anniversary Edition* (London and New York: Routledge, 2014), p. 30.

22. Mickey Lauria and Lawrence Knopp, 'Toward an Analysis of the Role of Gay Communities in the Urban Renaissance', *Urban Geography* 6.2 (1985): 152–69.

23. Brendan Kelly, 'Homosexuality and Irish Psychiatry: Medicine, Law and the Changing Face of Ireland', *Irish Journal of Psychological Medicine*, 34.3 (2017), pp. 209–15; Diarmaid Ferriter, *Occasions of Sin: Sex and Society in Modern Ireland* (London: Profile Books, 2009).

24. Manuel Castells, *The City and the Grassroots: A Cross-Cultural Theory of Urban Social Movements* (Berkeley: University of California Press, 1983), p. 138.

9. Defiance and Defence: The Gay Defence Committee, Police Harassment and the Murders of 1982

1. Oral history interview with Cathal Kerrigan.

2. Ibid.

3. Úna Mullally, 'Murder in Monkstown: The Brutal Killing of Charles Self', *The Irish Times*, 24 June 2017.

4. Ibid.

5. Dublin Lesbian and Gay Men's Collectives, *Out for Ourselves: The Lives of Irish Lesbians & Gay Men* (Dublin: Women's Community Press, 1986), p. 192.

6. Ibid.

7. Ibid.

8. For more on the work of Gays Against Imperialism see: Padraig Robinson, *Gaze Against Imperialism* (Sacramento, California: Metaflux, 2019); Maurice J. Casey, 'Radical Politics and Gay Activism in the Republic of Ireland, 1974–1990', *Irish Studies Review*, 26.2 (2018), pp. 217–36.

9. Patrick McDonagh, *Gay and Lesbian Activism in the Republic 1973–1993* (London and New York: Bloomsbury, 2021), p. 55; National Library of Ireland, IR 32341 G 24, Melissa Murray and Charles Kerrigan, 'Gays Step up the Pace', *Gralton*, 3 (August/September 1982), p. 5.

10. 'Man on Murder Charge Remanded', *The Irish Times*, 19 March 1982.

11. 'Murder Trial Told of Sexual Advances', *The Irish Times*, 21 October 1982.

12. Oral history interview with Cathal Kerrigan.

13. 'Late News', *Evening Herald*, 12 March 1982.

14. Oral history interview with Cathal Kerrigan.

15. 'Gardaí in Murder Hunt "Have Gays on File"', *Irish Press*, 25 March 1982.

16. Ibid.

17. Ibid.

18. Ibid.

19. Gay Defence Committee information leaflet, personal archive of Cathal Kerrigan.

20. Oral history interview with Cathal Kerrigan.

21. Peter Murtagh, 'Claim for Gay Rights Attacked', *The Irish Times*, 3 April 1982.

22. 'Man Didn't Admit Stabbing', *Evening Herald*, 13 May 1983.

23. 'Porter 'Killed over Homosexual Fears', *The Evening Press*, 11 May 1983.

10. 'Am I a Qualified-Enough Lesbian?' The Belfast Lesbian Line and Cross-Border Lesbian Solidarity

1. Oral history interview with Rita Wild.

2. Ibid.

3. Ibid.

4. Ibid.

5. Maureen Tatlow, 'All Go at the Belfast Lesbian Line', *Gay Community News*, issue 14, January 1990, p. 5.

6. Hugo McManus Collection, Irish Queer Archive, National Library of Ireland.

7. Cara-Friend Annual Report 1974–1975, Hibernica Collection, Special Collections & Archives, Queen's University Belfast.

8. Abigail Keating, 'From Partition to Decriminalisation: Homosexuality in Northern Ireland, 1921–1982', Creative Centenaries, 22 September 2021. Available at: https://creativecentenaries.org/blog/from-partition-to-decriminalisation-homosexuality-in-northern-ireland-1921-1982.

9. Jeff Dudgeon, 'Mapping 100 Years of Belfast Gay Life', *The Vacuum*, issue 11, 2006, p. 1.

10. Ibid.

11. Ibid.

12. Orla Egan, *Queer Republic of Cork: Cork's Lesbian, Gay, Bisexual and Transgender Communities, 1970s–1990s* (Cloghroe: Onstream, 2016), p. 53.

13. 'Help Us to Help You', *Gay Community News*, issue 41, July 1992, p. 16.

14. Oral history interview with Heather Fleming.

15. Cara-Friend Annual Report 1981–1982, Queen's University Belfast, Hibernica Collection, Special Collections & Archives, Queen's University Belfast.

16. Jack Crangle, Fearghus Roulston, Graham Dawson, Liam Harte and Barry Hazley, 'Somewhere Bigger and Brighter? Ambivalence

and Desire in Memories of Leaving the North of Ireland during the Troubles', *Irish Studies Review*, 30.3 (2022), p. 261.

17. Sean Brady, 'Ian Paisley (1926–2014) and the "Save Ulster from Sodomy!" Campaign', *Notches*, 16 September 2014. Available at: https://notchesblog.com/2014/09/16/ian-paisley-1926-2014-and-the-save-ulster-from-sodomy-campaign/.

18. Ibid.

19. Oral history interview with Heather Fleming.

20. Ibid.

21. Dudgeon, 'Mapping 100 Years of Belfast Gay Life'.

22. Oral history interview with Heather Fleming.

23. Jeff Dudgeon, 'A Century and More of Belfast Gay Life – Northern Ireland's Gay Geography, History and People: 1903–2020', AcomsDave, 23 October 2021. Available at: https://acomsdave.com/a-century-and-more-of-belfast-gay-life/.

24. Marian Duggan, *Queering Conflict: Examining Lesbian and Gay Experiences of Homophobia in Northern Ireland* (London and New York: Routledge, 2012), p. 63.

25. Oral history interview with Heather Fleming.

26. Ibid.

27. Oral history interview with Heather Fleming and Claire Hackett.

28. Oral history interview with Claire Hackett.

29. Ibid.

30. Marie Mulholland, 'Ghetto Blasting', in Íde O'Carroll and Eoin Collins (eds), *Lesbian and Gay Visions of Ireland: Towards the Twenty-First Century* (London: Cassell, 1995).

31. Oral history interview with Claire Hackett.

32. Jessica Toops, '"Living Lives of Quiet Desperation": Accounts of Gay Men and Lesbians During the Troubles', *Western Illinois Historical Review*, 6 (Spring 2014), p. 38.

33. Oral history interview with Claire Hackett.

34. Ibid.

35. 'Fun Weekend', *Munster GCN*, June 1993.

36. Egan, p. 48.

37. Derek Birrell and Amanda Hayes, *Cross Border Co-operation in Local Government: Models of Development, Management and Reconciliation*, May 2001. Available at: https://www.crossborder.ie/pubs/localgov.pdf.

38. Andrew O'Regan, 'Contexts and Constraints for NPOs: The Case of Co-Operation Ireland', *Voluntas: International Journal of Voluntary and Nonprofit Organization*, 12.3 (2001) p. 244.

39. Oral history interview with Rita Wild.

40. Oral history interview with Claire Hackett.

41. Ibid.

42. Ibid.

43. G. McCarthy, 'A New Line', *Women's Space*, issue 1, March 1988. Cork LGBT Archive, https://corklgbtarchive.com/items/show/59.

44. Ibid.

45. Ibid.

46. Cara-Friend Annual Report 1988–1989, Queen's University Belfast, Hibernica Collection, Special Collections & Archives, Queen's University Belfast.

47. Oral history interview with Rita Wild.

11. Pride in Parenting: Toni Burgess and the Story of Lesbian and Gay Parenting Rights

1. Oral history interview with Toni Burgess.

2. Ibid.

3. Tonie Walsh, 'It's a Sin: An Irish Perspective on the Superb TV Drama about Gay Life in the 1980s', *The Irish Examiner*, 10 February 2022.

4. 'Gay Rights: It's Time', information leaflet, Gay Pride Week 1980.

5. Oral history interview with Eamon Somers.

6. Dublin Lesbian and Gay Men's Collectives, *Out for Ourselves: The Lives of Irish Lesbians and Gay Men* (Dublin: Women's Community Press, 1986).

7. Ibid., p. 64.

8. Ibid., p. 65.

9. Ibid.

10. Oral history interview with Pauline O'Donnell.

11. Oral history interview with Rita Wild.

12. Gillian Hanscombe, 'The Right to Lesbian Parenthood', *Journal of Medical Ethics*, 9 (1983), pp. 133–5.

13. Nancy Polikoff, 'Lesbian Mothers, Lesbian Families: Legal Obstacles, Legal Challenges', *New York University Review of Law & Social Change*, 14.4 (2021), p. 907.

14. Ibid.

15. Annette Hoctor, 'Children: Whose Right to Choose?', in Dublin Lesbian and Gay Men's Collectives, p. 66.

16. Oral history interview with Toni Burgess.

17. Ibid.

18. Quay Co-op, Cork, '1982 Quay Co-op Document', Cork LGBT Archive.

19. Orla Egan, 'Trailblazing Cork Quay Co-op Celebrates 40th Birthday', *Gay Community News*, 24 May 2022. Available at: https://gcn.ie/cork-quay-co-op-40-years-existence/.

20. Orla Egan and Megan Luddy O'Leary, *Diary of an Activist* (Cork: Cork City Libraries, 2022).

21. Oral history interview with Toni Burgess.

22. Ibid.

23. Ibid.

24. Ibid.

25. Ibid.

26. 'The Campaign', Equality for Children. Available at: https://equality-forchildren.ie/campaign; Páraic Kerrigan and Amber Cushing, '"Our Story with the State": Birth Certificates, Data Structures and Gay and Lesbian Families', *Sexualities*, 10 June 2022.

12. Out at Work? Louise Hannon, Transgender Rights and Employment Equality

1. Oral history interview with Louise Hannon.

2. Oral history interview with Derek Byrne.

3. Ibid.

4. Orla Egan, *Queer Republic of Cork: Cork's Lesbian, Gay, Bisexual and Transgender Communities, 1970s–1990s* (Cloghroe: Onstream, 2016), p. 81.

5. 'Prima!Donna', *Munster Lesbian and Gay Community News*, March 1994.

6. Ibid.

7. Anita Whooley, 'Out and Proud of It!', *Irish Examiner*, 23 February 1994.

8. 'Coffee at Brookfield', *Southern Star*, 19 February 1994.

9. Government of Ireland, Employment Equality Act 1998. Available at https://www.irishstatutebook.ie/eli/1998/act/21/enacted/en/html

10. Ciarán Ó hUltacháin, 'Taylor May Make Changes to Employment Equality Bill', *Gay Community News*, issue 90, November 1996. p. 1.

11. Michael Cronin, 'Section 37 in "Bill of Inequality"', *Gay Community News*, issue 96, June 1997.

12. Declan Fahie, '"Spectacularly Exposed and Vulnerable" – How Irish Equality Legislators Subverted the Personal and Professional Security of Lesbian, Gay and Bisexual Teachers', *Sexualities*, 19.4 (2016), pp. 393–411.

13. These two quotes are taken from Declan Fahie's article, cited above, which includes quotations from interviews with LGB teachers who have been anonymised and de-identified in the article.

14. Oral history interview with Louise Hannon.

15. Andrew Sharpe, 'English Transgender Law Reform and the *Spectre* of Corbett', *Feminist Legal Studies*, 10.6 (2002), pp. 5–89.

16. Oral history interview with Louise Hannon.

17. 'The Thrill of the Change', *The Irish Times*, 22 October 1997.

18. Oral history interview with Louise Hannon.

19. *Hannon v First Direct Logistics Limited*, File No. EE/2008/04. Date of Issue: 29 March 2011.

20. Ibid.

21. Ibid.

22. Ibid.

23. Ibid.

24. Ibid.

25. Oral history interview with Louise Hannon.

26. Michael Farrell, 'Lydia Foy and the Struggle for Gender Recognition: A Case Study in Public Interest Litigation', *Socio-Legal Studies Review*, 1 (2015), pp. 153–9.

27. Ibid.

28. Transgender Equality Network Ireland (TENI), 'Supporting Transgender Inclusion in the Workplace: Guidelines for Employers and Employees', 2017. Available at: https://teni.ie/reports/.

29. Amber L. Cushing and Páraic Kerrigan, 'Extending the PIM-B Concept: An Exploration of How Nonbinary People Maintain Personal Information Over Time', in Isaac Sserwanga et al. (eds), *Information for a Better World: Normality, Virtuality, Physicality, Inclusivity*, iConference 2023, Lecture Notes in Computer Science, vol. 13971 (Cham: Springer, 2023). https://doi.org/10.1007/978-3-031-28035-1_10.

30. Oral history interview with Louise Hannon.

13. Indecent and Most Obscene: Censorship and Suppression in Queer Irish Culture

1. Based on Edmund Lynch's interview with Terri Blanche, 17 June 2013, Irish LGBT Oral History Project.

2. Donal Ó'Drisceoil, '"The Best Banned in the Land": Censorship and Irish Writing Since 1950', *The Yearbook of English Studies*, 35 (2005), pp. 146–60.

3. Ibid.

4. Government of Ireland, Censorship of Publications Act, 1929. Available at: https://www.irishstatutebook.ie/eli/1929/act/21/enacted/en/print.

5. Peter Martin, 'Irish Censorship in Context', *Studies: An Irish Quarterly Review*, 95.379 (2006), pp. 261–8.

6. Michael G. Cronin, 'Kate O'Brien and the Erotics of Liberal Catholic Dissent', *Field Day Review* (2010), p. 6.

7. Kate O'Brien, *The Land of Spices* (London: Virago, 2011), p. 165.

8. 'Queer Ireland: Broderick, *The Pilgrimage* (1961)', *Censored* podcast. Available at: http://censored.ie/queer-ireland-broderick/.

9. Julia Carlson, 'Still Censored after All These Years', *The Irish Times*, 11 June 1991.

10. National Library of Ireland, Irish Queer Archives, Box MS 45, 948/9.

11. Ruth Riddick, 'The Book', *Gay Community News*, issue 22, September 1990, p. 10.

12. Lorna Siggins, 'Controversial British Book on Homosexuality Banned', *The Irish Times*, 30 July 1990.

13. Ibid.

14. Chris Macey, 'Gay Anger as Censor Bans Book for Children', *The Evening Press*, 30 July 1990.

15. Ibid.

16. Kieran Rose, 'Open Letter', *Gay Community News*, issue 22, September 1990, p. 5.

17. GCN Editorial response to Kieran Rose's open letter, *Gay Community News*, issue 22, September 1990, p. 5.

18. Margaret McWilliam, 'Family Solidarity Book "Fascist" Says Councillor', *Gay Community News*, issue 22, September 1990, p. 1.

19. Frank Thackaberry, 'Outwaves', *Gay Community News*, issue 23, October 1990, p. 4.

20. GCN Reporter, 'Outwaves Threat to Silence Programme', *Gay Community News*, issue 24, November 1990, p. 1.

21. 'Editorial – The Beast of Bigotry', *OUT*, issue 15, 1988.

22. Andy Pollak, 'AIDS Ad Refused by RTÉ Guide', *The Irish Times*, 22 November 1986.

23. Ibid.

24. Mark V. Healy, 'Too Hot to Handle!' *Gay Community News*, issue 43, August 1992, p. 4.

25. Audrey Magee, 'Anger at RTÉ AIDS Ad Ban', *The Irish Times*, 18 May 1993.

26. Ibid.

27. Ibid.

14. Beyond Convention: Alternative Miss Ireland's Trailblazing Odyssey (1987–2012)

1. Lurleen, 'New York State of Mind', *Alternative Miss Ireland: Dancing at the Crossroads* (Dublin: X Communications, 2004), p. 106.

2. Ibid.

3. Oral history interview with Davina Devine.

4. Panti Bliss, 'Babies!' *Alternative Miss Ireland: Dancing at the Crossroads* (Dublin: X Communications, 2004) p. 32.

5. Niall Sweeney, 'Alternative Miss Ireland: Dancing at the Crossroads – Glamour Rooted in Despair', Presentation given at University College Dublin, 2022.

6. Frank Stanley, 'Illiberated', *Alternative Miss Ireland: Dancing at the Crossroads* (Dublin: X Communications, 2004), p. 19.

7. Tonie Walsh, 'Running on Overdrive …' *Alternative Miss Ireland: Dancing at the Crossroads* (Dublin: X Communications, 2004), p. 21.

8. Stanley.

9. Han Tiernan, 'Remembering Ireland's Iconic Drag Spectacular Alternative Miss Ireland', *Gay Community News*. Available at: https://gcn.ie/remembering-alternative-miss-ireland-part-1/.

10. Oral history interview with Noel Sutton.

11. Oral history interview with Tonie Walsh.

12. Oral history interview with Katherine Lynch.

13. Ibid.

14. Ailbhe Smyth, 'Ms. Veda, the Mogul and Me', *Alternative Miss Ireland: Dancing at the Crossroads* (Dublin: X Communications, 2004), p. 61.

15. Oral history interview with Katherine Lynch.

16. Fintan Walsh, *Queer Performance and Contemporary Ireland: Dissent and Disorientation* (London and New York: Palgrave, 2016), p. 22.

17. Sinéad Burke, 'It's Never Too Early for Children to Learn to Be Curious and Kind', *The Irish Times*, 24 October 2020. Available at: https://www.irishtimes.com/life-and-style/health-family/sinead-burke-it-s-never-too-early-for-children-to-learn-to-be-curious-and-kind-1.4379795.

18. Minnie Mélange, 'Minnie's Pride', *Gay Community News*, issue 283, 2013, p. 16.

19. 'Minnie Mélange/Sinéad Burke', *Róisín Meets* podcast, 9 May 2015. Available at: https://www.irishtimes.com/life-and-style/people/roisin-meets-sinead-burke-on-life-as-a-little-person-1.2205295.

20. Oral history interview with Noel Sutton.

21. Ibid.

22. Ibid.

Index